D0207879

# TEACHER POLITICS

**Recent Titles in**
**Contributions to the Study of Education**

# TEACHER POLITICS

## The Influence of Unions

## MAURICE R. BERUBE

CONTRIBUTIONS TO THE STUDY OF EDUCATION,
NUMBER 26

Greenwood Press
NEW YORK · WESTPORT, CONNECTICUT · LONDON

Library of Congress Cataloging-in-Publication Data

Berube, Maurice R.
    Teacher politics: the influence of unions / Maurice R. Berube.
        p. cm.—(Contributions to the study of education, ISSN
    0196-707X ; no. 26)
    Bibliography: p.
    Includes index.
    ISBN 0-313-25685-3 (lib. bdg. : alk. paper)
    1. Teachers' unions—United States.   2. National Education
Association of the United States.   3. American Federation of
Teachers.   4. Teachers—United States—Political activity.
I. Title.   II. Series.
LB2844.53.U6B47   1988
331.88′113711′00973—dc19                                87-29546


British Library Cataloguing in Publication Data is available.

Library of Congress Catalog Card Number: 87-29546
ISBN: 0-313-25685-3
ISSN: 0196-707X

First published in 1988

Greenwood Press, Inc.
88 Post Road West, Westport, Connecticut 06881

Printed in the United States of America

The paper used in this book complies with the
Permanent Paper Standard issued by the National
Information Standards Organization (Z39.48-1984).

10 9 8 7 6 5 4 3 2 1

For those teachers who made a difference:
    Brother Patrick of Mount St. Michael's, New York City,
    Mary Hamilton of Lewiston High School, Lewiston, Maine,
    Professors Robert M. Brown, Robert V. Remini, and
    Robert Pollock of Fordham University,

And to my uncle, the late Professor Ralph L. Bérubé of Fordham
    University, who encouraged me to attend college.

# Contents

# Preface

The idea to write this book was the result of preparing a class on the politics of education at Old Dominion University. I could find no scholarly study of the key actors in the politics of education, namely, the National Education Association (NEA) and the American Federation of Teachers (AFT), AFL-CIO. Since my interest and background in teacher unionism was longstanding, I decided to write a study of the teacher unions in politics.

Not only have I followed the development of teacher unionism for three decades, but I have been active as a teacher unionist. As a schoolteacher in the 1950s and 1960s, I was a chapter chairman for my school with the United Federation of Teachers (UFT), AFL-CIO, the New York City affiliate of the AFT. Moreover, I subsequently became an editor with that teacher union for three years from 1964 to 1967. At that time, the union employed two full-time staff members as state political lobbyists.

Despite my asssociation with the UFT, I do not believe that this study is victim to narrow partisanship. After leaving the UFT, I found myself opposing the union in the struggle for community control in the sixties-elected, city school boards—a position vigorously attacked by the UFT. At the time, I was a staff member of the Institute for Community Studies at Queens College, a conduit for experiments in community control. With the director of the institute, Professor Marilyn Gittell, I co-authored three books, two of them studies dealing with elected, urban school boards. My attitude toward teacher unions can best be described as sympathetic but nonetheless critical.

A number of people provided assistance in the preparation of this book. John O'Neill, former Director of Staff of the United Federation of Teachers, furnished critical material as did Judy Baum, Director of Information for the Public Education Association. The staffs of both the NEA and AFT at all levels, local, state and national, were extremely helpful. My son, Michael Berube, a doctoral student at the University of Virginia, was able to secure at that school's library important periodicals not available to me. And Professor James Henry, chairman of the Department of Educational Leadership at Old Dominion University, provided needed financial assistance for travel in interviewing key union staff members.

Several people were kind enough to read the manuscript and offer suggestions. Mickey Ibarra, Dale Lestina and Joseph Standa of the NEA political action staff read chapter 2 on the NEA for accuracy. Former president of the AFT David Selden reviewed the entire manuscript. Professors William Cunningham and Joseph P. Mooney of Old Dominion University also read the manuscript in preparation and made pertinent comments. I am grateful to them for their interest and their aid.

I would be remiss if I did not acknowledge an intellectual debt. Professor Paul Starr's monumental work, *The Social Transformation of American Medicine* served as a model and suggested what could happen, perhaps, for the teaching profession.

I must express my deep gratitude to the editors at Greenwood Press. Dr. James Sabin, vice president, has continued his support and my editor, Loomis Mayer, was considerate and skillful. The production editors have been extremely thoughtful. Special mention must be made of Trisha Taylor's fine copyediting.

And David Selden, former AFT president and a friend for over a generation, influenced me in his two decades of advocacy of a merger for the two teacher unions.

Nevertheless, I must accept final responsibility for this analysis. It has truly been a labor of love.

# TEACHER POLITICS

# 1

# Teachers in Politics

Teachers are a powerful force in American politics. Through their huge organizations—the National Education Association (NEA) with 1.8 million members, and the American Federation of Teachers (AFT) with 600,000 members—this force of nearly 2.5 million teachers is changing American educational politics. This is being done by means of powerful lobbying arms seeking favored legislation and political machines supporting local, state and national candidates with manpower and money. Indeed, the editors of the respected education journal *Phi Delta Kappan*, the educators' bible, proclaimed the rise of teacher politics as "the most astonishing story of our time."[1]

The main thesis of this study is that the teacher unions have become the most powerful political constituency in education. Because of their enormous resources, their natural interest in education and the transitory nature of parent and student support, teacher unions have become the chief representatives of education in American politics.

On balance, the teacher unions have been reasonably effective in their political and legislative endeavors. They have successfully supported mayors, governors and state legislators, members of Congress and even one president of the United States. They have reaped the rewards of their political endorsements by having much of their legislative program adopted and by stopping much that has been opposed. However, their power has not been absolute. On occasion, union-supported candidates have lost. That has occurred most notably in the last two presidential elections.

However, the two teacher unions differ markedly in some educational goals as well as other social and political objectives. In the past generation, the NEA, ironically, has moved from a promoter of the status quo to a politically liberal position. By contrast, the AFT, which long espoused a liberal—and sometimes radical—agenda, moved slightly to the right of center. Although both unions remained in the Democratic party camp, for the most part, the philosophical differences have often resulted in the NEA and AFT supporting opposing candidates.

As a corollary to the main thesis, the teacher unions have, unfortunately, been reactive to school reform. In the 1960s, the civil rights movement ushered in the equity school reform wave. In the 1980s, competition from Japan and other free industrialized nations prompted politicians to initiate the "excellence" school reform movement that shifted the focus from educating the disadvantaged to educating the best and brightest. The teacher unions proved followers, and sometimes reluctant ones at that.

Finally, it is argued that the teacher unions may only become initiators of sweeping change when they become unified into one organization. The competition between the unions for members has blunted their educational effectiveness. Regrettably, the prospect for one big teacher union that would be the cutting edge of educational and social change appears unlikely in the near future.

## THE RISE OF TEACHER POLITICS

The teacher unions have become involved in politics only during the last generation. Although the NEA and AFT had long maintained lobbying efforts, it wasn't until the mid-1960s that political action committees supporting candidates were formed on a local level and until the early 1970s when they were created on a national union level. It is this past generation of educational tumult that we shall examine in this study.

Moreover, teacher politics was the result of the breakthrough in collective bargaining. With the ability to negotiate union contracts and the widespread teacher rebellion that ensued, it was but one short step to consider political involvement. After the collective bargaining breakthrough in New York City in 1961, the teacher rebellion resulted in dramatic membership gains. The NEA grew from 703,829 members in 1957, to 1,709,693 in 1979.[2] The AFT followed suit, going from 136,000 members in 1967, to 600,000 today.[3]

The rationale for entering politics was a logical progression from union growth. School budgets were determined by local, state and congressional officials. Public agencies controlled by elected politicians determined the course of public education in America. Union leaders concluded that they must act beyond the domain of collective bargaining. In order to achieve their legislative goals, teachers needed to become politically involved and support candidates in the same way as did teachers' professional brethren, physicians and lawyers. However, the development of a political consciousness throughout the leadership or the rank and file did not come about immediately, and there was some resistance.

Teacher organizations now possess enormous human and financial resources. Teachers vote in overwhelming numbers and actively participate as campaign workers. In the 1980 presidential campaign, for example, one observer claimed that the NEA enlisted 500,000 teacher volunteers working on behalf of their candidate, President Jimmy Carter.[4] The NEA also boasts more money—some $375 million more—than the entire labor movement.[5] Among contributions to federal candidates, the NEA is the fifth largest benefactor, two notches behind the American Medical Association, whose members have the highest incomes in the United States.[6] Few organizations carry the clout of the teacher unions.

The NEA has become a political giant, and the AFT is closely following suit. For example, in the 1980 presidential campaign, 464 delegates and alternates to the Democratic convention were NEA delegates—one-tenth of all delegates, and one in seven of Carter delegates.[7] The NEA support of Carter was deemed crucial in stemming the challenge of the AFT-backed Senator Edward Kennedy. In 1974, two years after forming a Political Action Committee, NEA officials could boast that 229 of 282 NEA-endorsed candidates won election in the House of Representatives, and twenty-two of twenty-eight candidates won in the Senate.[8] Perhaps the greatest NEA victory has been in 1976 when the organization successfully supported a presidential candidate for the first time:

Jimmy Carter. It was with great pride that former NEA President John Ryor could proclaim that "we can elect friends of education and un-elect foes."[9]

The AFT has shown its political muscle on a national level as well, although not having the enormous financial resources of the NEA. In the 1984 national elections, the AFT contributed nearly three-quarters of a million dollars. Of that sum, $278,415 went for House and Senate candidates, and $170,000 was contributed to the Democratic Senate Committee, Democratic National and State parties.[10] The AFL-CIO also received a substantial AFT contribution of $262,000 for the 1984 election.[11]

But the teacher unions are not only politically strong in national elections. They are especially influential on a state level and are also instrumental in local elections. State politics is of strategic importance. Because the founding fathers neglected to mention education in the Constitution, education is a state responsibility in America; therefore, state legislatures determine, by and large, educational policies. Consequently, the teacher unions are extremely active in state politics. In New York State, for example, the one AFT-dominated state, more than a half million dollars for state political activity was raised in 1984.[12] The New York State United Teachers AFL-CIO maintains seven full-time lobbyists and six employees working on political activities.[13] The California Teachers Association (NEA) is considered the second richest lobby behind the oil companies and helped elect all but three of the fifty-four Democratic State Assemblymen in 1974.[14]

Another development has been the entry of former teachers and professors into political life. This trend is increasingly pronounced on federal, state and local levels. United States voters have elected one president of the United States, Woodrow Wilson, who was a college professor, and another president, Lyndon Johnson, who was a schoolteacher. Indeed, Johnson's tenure, with Vice President Hubert Humphrey, a former college professor as vice president, marked a high in teacher-politics. Moreover, these two men ascended to high office precisely at the moment of a large-scale educational reform movement that had been spurred by the civil rights movement. The result was that more educational legislation was passed than ever, and, finally, a federal aid to education law was enacted.

In Congress there has recently been a notable presence of former educators. By 1986, in the 99th Congress, there were seven United States Senators and twenty-eight Representatives in the House with teaching backgrounds. In the Senate, all but one of the seven were from higher education. In the House, eighteen of the twenty-eight were from schoolteaching backgrounds, with ten former college professors. In the Senate, five of the seven with such backgrounds were Republican and two were Democrats. Senator Daniel Patrick Moynihan (D-N.Y.) for example, was a former college professor who enjoyed a national academic reputation. In the House, eighteen members with teaching backgrounds were Democrats and nine were Republicans. This sample of congressional members from education mirrored the political makeup of the 99th Congress: The Senate had a Republican majority (as were most of the educationally associated Senators); and the House had a Democratic majority (as were its educationally associated Representatives).[15]

On a state level, Alan Rosenthal and Susan Fuhrman discovered in their study on legislative educational leadership that most legislative leaders in education were former teachers or school administrators. What is meant by *legislative leader* is that person who exerts strong influence through his or her position on educational legislation. Rosenthal and Fuhrman found that of the leaders surveyed among all the state legislatures in the nation, 43 percent had been teachers.[16] This state experience corresponds with that of the U.S. Congress where many former educators devote themselves to the cause of education.

## THE CONTROVERSY

Politics engenders controversy. It would be inevitable that the teacher unions would be criticized for their political involvement. Their liberal social philosophies conflicted with a resurgent conservative movement in the mid-1970s. Moreover, there was additional fallout: polls indicated that parents were increasingly negative to the profession of teaching. Finally, there was the larger question of whether political action committees representing special interests were good for the body politic.

The controversy that erupted over the entry of teachers into politics followed liberal-conservative political lines. Essentially, the furor arose over the NEA's endorsement of Jimmy Carter for president in 1976. Prior to that time, there had been little criticism of what teacher involvement there was in politics. But the NEA's endorsement of Carter was historic; it was the first time that the NEA had ever supported a presidential candidate. Although the AFT had previously supported Senator George McGovern for the presidency in 1972, critics of the teacher organizations were more perturbed by the NEA action. That upset can be partially explained by the fact that the NEA was the larger association, three times that of the AFT. Equally important, the NEA had begun a process of drifting to the political left in the 1970s, whereas the AFT was moving to the right of center at a time when the political mood of the nation was growing increasingly conservative. Consequently, conservative critics almost wholly centered their attacks on the NEA.

The criticisms of the NEA were varied. NEA members were accused of being captives of the Democratic party, hostile to the capitalist economy, against the preservation of the family, soft on communism, and, finally, detrimental to the best interests of education, by promoting a negative image of teachers. Few critics mentioned the possible divisive effects that support of specific candidates would have on membership and teacher unity.

On the conservative side of the ledger were such publications as the *Reader's Digest, National Review,* and the neo-conservative magazine *Commentary.* For the most part, this discussion was confined to journals of opinion with small circulations and educational magazines. However, the controversy spilled over to such mass magazines as *Time* and the *Reader's Digest,* with circulations in the millions. Ironically, the most bitter attack came in the pages of the *New Republic,* historically a liberal journal, which in recent years has become conservative on certain issues and therefore characterizes itself as "neo-liberal" (defined as "conservative Democrats"). Even the educationally cautious *Phi Delta Kappan* described the NEA's political activities as "callous."[17] Only in the historically liberal-left journal *The Nation* did the NEA receive support for its position.

*Reader's Digest* sought to warn its readers of the NEA as a Washington lobby run rampant. Eugene H. Methvin characterized the NEA's endorsement of Carter for president in 1976 as a signal for a "drive for power, nationwide," which would result in "special-interest politics" that would "overwhelm the public interest."[18] Methvin questioned whether teacher politics was "really in the best interests of teachers."[19] What Methvin objected to, without stating it, was that the NEA supported a candidate not to his liking.

Replying to the *Reader's Digest* article, Terry Herndon, former Executive Secretary of the NEA, noted that the "NEA has longed for universal citizen participation in politics" and that "educators want and need a politically active citizenry."[20] Confronting the charge that the NEA was not acting in the public interest, Herndon countered that the diversity of NEA members was "uncommon and may well make NEA the politically active group which is most representative of America."[21] He perceived Methvin's unstated intent on writing the article and concluded:

Finally we come to the bottom line. The *Reader's Digest* article is not so much a report of NEA's political effort but rather a statement of disagreement with the substance of that effort. We seek an expanded federal responsibility for the support of state and local efforts to provide educational opportunities. *Reader's Digest* opposes this effort and strives to identify the position with the public interest. We obviously disagree and find our effort to be in the public interest.[22]

Russell Kirk, writing in the *National Review*, the journal of American conservatism, was more candid. For him, Ronald Reagan was "keenly interested in improving the quality of American public instruction," whereas "the notion is anathema to the bosses of the NEA."[23] According to Kirk, the NEA was opposed not only to educational progress but also was "intensely hostile toward the private sector" and "repeats like incantations many of the shallow slogans of the New Left."[24] And if that wasn't bad enough, the NEA's promotion of early schooling and day care seemed tantamount to attempting "to replace the social functions of the family."[25]

But it was left to the pages of the neo-conservative magazine *Commentary* to escalate the attack. The NEA leadership could even be accused of being unpatriotic. Chester Finn, Jr., then an education professor and later in President Reagan's Department of Education, charged that the NEA had maintained a generally "uncritical stance toward Moscow."[26] What disturbed Finn most, however, was that both teacher unions were "firmly in the Democratic camp," which means that "Republicans rarely owe debts or favors to the teacher unions."[27] This has, according to Finn, created a vicious circle. Republican platforms "now pay little heed to teacher interests" since education has now been labeled a "Democratic concern."[28]

The *New Republic*, a journal for neo-liberals described the NEA as "the most powerful special interest group in Washington."[29] The NEA's seizure of power, according to Associate Editor Stephen Chapman, bodes ill for American education.

If you think that all this newfound power will be deployed for benevolent purposes, think again here too. The NEA has only one purpose: to further the interest of teachers. It has made clear that the interests of teachers and the interests of education don't necessarily coincide. . . . All these gains may be good for teachers but they're likely to be bad for American education.[30]

Perhaps the unkindest cut of all came in the *Phi Delta Kappan*. Despite regularly publishing articles imploring education to close the gap with politics, Stanley E. Elam, longtime former editor, excoriated the NEA for playing "callous pressure politics" which will prevent it from reaching its goals through "the ultimately self-defeating special-interest game, the bane of modern American politics."[31] Only in the liberal journal *Nation* did journalist Brian Sullam hail "the massive politicization of teachers" as being "one of the most substantial developments" in politics.[32]

Surprisingly the AFT has been spared criticism. That has been due mostly to the movement of the AFT toward a slightly right of center position on both educational and social issues. Methvin in the *Reader's Digest* would gloat that the AFT "opposes the NEA on virtually every educational-reform issue."[33] Elam writing in *Phi Delta Kappan* would describe AFT President Albert Shanker as "cool and articulate," a person who evinces "real anguish" when mulling the difficulties of merging with the NEA.[34]

It was inevitable that a book critical of the NEA—"the first full-length exposé of the National Education Association"—should be published. In late 1984, two months before the November presidential elections, conservative writer Samuel L. Blumenfeld would have his *NEA: Trojan Horse in American Education* published by the new Paradigm Company of Boise, Idaho. Blumenfeld, a graduate of City College in New York City, had been a teacher in both public and private schools. His sympathy is clearly with the latter, and one of the major recommendations of his book is to "let every child get a good private education."[35] In that fashion, a "nation at risk" would "change overnight into a nation of achievement."[36]

Blumenfeld's polemic on the NEA was essentially political. American teachers, he said were "being trained and manipulated by the NEA to bring socialism to America."[37] He charged that the NEA was "little more than the socialist Trojan horse within our political walls."[38] The aim of his book was to show that teachers are "no longer the benign, neutral servants of our communities" and that they "are being used by clever political activists to bring the radical left to power."[39] Students are obtaining "heavy doses of propaganda from their politicized teachers."[40] In his broadside, Blumenfeld melded the new political strength of the NEA with its social and educational goals and concluded:

The NEA is probably the most intellectually dishonest organization in America. It is part union, part professional organization, and part political party. Its object is to control the Congress, the fifty state legislatures, the Democratic Party, the curriculum in all the schools, public and private, and the entire teaching profession. Its interest in academics is subordinate to its radical political and social ends.[41]

The conservative opposition to the NEA's influence, however, was not restricted to books and magazines. A grassroots lobby called Save Our Schools founded in 1980 by Dan C. Alexander, Jr., mobilized a significant number of supporters and raised a substantial sum of money. By the spring of 1985, Save Our Schools counted some 150,000 supporters in fifty states and an operating budget of $1,626,000. Save Our Schools "believes the National Education Association (NEA) Teacher Union is a threat to traditional moral values and educational standards of the United States."[42] Alexander, a former president of the school board in Mobile, Alabama,

has concluded that the NEA is dominated by educational and political radicals who hold too much power. He characterized the
organization as follows:

The NEA is a militant teacher union dominated and run by a hard core
group of radical educators. They are intent on reshaping America through
our public schools. It is the *single most powerful force* in public education, today. . . . The NEA is run by an ultra-liberal group of educators
who are more interested in changing America's values and politics than
educating her children. . . . The NEA has become a powerful force in
public education today. In fact, I don't believe it's an exaggeration to say
the NEA has more influence on education at all levels than any other
group in the nation . . . *national, state, and local.*[43]

Save Our Schools maintains a conservative educational and political philosophy removed from the "ultra-liberal" NEA, which is
"far away" from the "traditional values most Americans believe in."[44]
Save Our Schools describes itself as a "grassroots lobbying organization that supports a return to the 'basics' in education" and "with
more emphasis on fundamentals (and) greater student discipline."[45] Save Our Schools supports competency testing of teachers, abolition of the Department of Education, and school prayer.

In addition to the growing political influence of the NEA, Alexander especially objected to NEA's social philosophy. He listed six
key beliefs of the NEA that particularly rankle Save Our Schools:
supporting homosexuality (especially by having homosexuals teach),
abortion, busing for school integration, nuclear freeze, opposing
prayer in the schools and anti-communism in Central America.

Alexander circulated an opinion survey in the spring of 1985 that
would be a basis for a major television investigative report on the
NEA. The third of seven survey questions asked: "Should teacher
unions be involved in politics, support candidates and run political
campaigns?"[46] The survey was sent to conservative supporters with
the request to contribute funds to the proposed television project.
The target figure was $380,000 to produce a television "documen-
tary." Professional producers were approached to create the show
to be titled "The NEA—Prescription for Disaster." Alexander reasoned that using a television show would be the best manner for
combating the NEA's "conspiracy to radically take over American

public education" because *"in America today there is nothing more powerful than television."*[47]

Just as predictably, the NEA responded to its conservative critics. In March 1985, the NEA published a small booklet titled *The Radical Right Attack on the National Education Association*. The NEA identified thirty-one charges that were "the most common and outrageous misinterpretations of NEA policy" ranging from its position on homosexual teachers to nuclear war.[48] The NEA identified its chief critics as extremists, radical right fringe groups, that seek to "characterize NEA as part of a Marxist conspiracy to destroy America."[49] To the contrary, the NEA claimed to be "in America's ideological mainstream" rather than "far to the left of its members."[50] According to the NEA, it is a target because it advocates "more effectively and relentlessly for public education than any other organization" and is "an obstacle to the Radical Right agenda."[51] That agenda is simply to: "impose a new political, religious, and social order on our nation, an order that unquestionably accepts ultraconservative views on everything from foreign policy to the textbooks in our classrooms."[52]

Four charges addressed by the NEA are political. The first is that NEA has become "unprofessional" when members became involved in politics.[53] The NEA pointed out that public school budgets and educational standards are politically controlled and require input from educators. Most important, NEA is setting an example when its members get involved in politics: "Good citizenship in a democracy *requires* participation in the political process."[54] Second, the NEA denied it is a "captive of the Democratic Party" but has a policy where "NEA works for and supports friends of education regardless of party affiliation."[55] The last two political charges involved a denial by the NEA that it uses dues for political activities and that it has a "hit list" of political opponents the organization seeks to defeat.

### A Negative Image of Teachers

There is some evidence that suggests public disenchantment with teachers. That disillusionment seems to be a result of the changing image of teachers. When former NEA Executive Director Terry Herndon proclaimed that the decision to enter politics meant that teachers were "not considered nice, quiet Milquetoasts anymore" he signalled the change.[56]

What has been the reaction of the public? Not as many parents want their children to become teachers as they once had. In a 1984 Gallup Poll conducted for *Phi Delta Kappan*, only 50 percent of parents of daughters and 47 percent of parents of sons considered teaching a notable career.[57] Fifteen years earlier, 75 percent of parents believed that teaching was a worthwhile profession.[58] The decline in teacher salaries during the 1970s seems to have had little effect on the decision of parents not to encourage their children to be teachers. In 1969, 43 percent believed that teacher salaries were adequate whereas in 1984, 41 percent believed that teacher salaries were "about right"—a decline of only 2 percent, a rather negligible figure.[59] One must surmise that the changing image of teachers has had some influence on parents choices. Indeed, concern appears to be more on the new image of the teacher as one of an aggressive union member exerting political influence.

Of real concern is the decline in the talent pool of teachers in recent years. Education majors have scored dismally on standardized tests. These majors rank low among major occupational groups on the Scholastic Aptitude Tests (SAT) and the Graduate Record Examination (GRE). Of sixteen occupational groups prospective teachers score fourteenth on the SAT verbal and sixteenth, last, in the quantitative.[60]

There may be a correlation between a less academically strong talent pool and the decline in teacher salaries. In absolute terms of purchasing power, the average salary of teachers peaked in 1973 and declined by $1,000 in 1980, while inflation bolstered salaries in competing fields.[61]

The public appears sympathetic to the teachers' plight. A Gallup Poll commissioned by the NEA in 1985 revealed that 63 percent considered higher teacher salaries the most important measure to improve education and 59 percent were willing to pay for those increases through higher taxes.[62] Moreover, indications are that the raising of salaries has enticed former teachers to return to the classroom. An AFT survey conducted in 1986 (after teacher salaries were increased by 23 percent nationwide) reported that former teachers returned to the classroom. In New Jersey, 64.3 percent

of new teachers were former teachers, and in Connecticut the percentage was 58.1 percent.[63]

## PAC POLITICS

A larger controversy has developed over the dominance of
American politics by special interest groups, of which the NEA
and AFT political action committees (PACs) constitute one. Critics
of the PACs contend that special interest groups with large amounts
of money unduly influence American politics. They claim that the
public does not desire special interest group politics, that the PACs
make campaigns excessively expensive, that usually incumbents are
supported, and that in many cases contributors have no say on
whom the PAC supports. Public opinion polls do indicate that
Americans disapprove of PACs. But those polled also indicated that
they should be able to contribute to an organization that supports
candidates.[64]

One of the most dramatic occurrences in American politics has
been the proliferation of PACs in the last decade. The first was
created by the Congress of Industrial Organizations (CIO), a labor
group, in 1943.[65] By 1972, there were 113 PACs; a decade later
there would be 3,525 PACs.[66]

As a result of the proliferation of PACs, campaigns have become
more expensive. PAC money has allowed candidates to devote a
good share of campaign costs to costly television. PAC money in
congressional races skyrocketed from $12 million in 1974 to $104
million in 1984.[67]

Moreover, PACs tend to support incumbents. The reasoning is
that PACs do not want to waste money on challengers when the
incumbents always win and stay in Congress some length of time.
Most important, many PACs make the decisions on who to support
without input from contributors.

Still, there seems to be little alternative in interest group politics. Professor Larry Sabato, who has studied PACs closely, believes that PACs are here to stay despite their lack of popularity
with "idealistic reformers" because they represent "the rough, cutting edge of democracy teeming with different peoples and conflicting interests."[68] In 1986, the Senate voted by a 69–30 tally to

limit PAC contributions to $3,000 per candidate down from $5,000.[69] The Senate, however, composed of all incumbents, tied the vote to a bill that had little chance of passage. It is unlikely that PACs will be eliminated.

## NOTES

1. *Phi Delta Kappan*, October 1976, p. 153.

2. Allan M. West, *The National Education Association: The Power Base for Education* (New York: Free Press, 1980), p. 38.

3. Stephen Chapman, "The Teachers' Coup," *New Republic*, October 11, 1980, p. 9.

4. George Neill, "NEA: New Powerhouse in the Democratic Party," *Phi Delta Kappan*, October 1980, p. 85.

5. Eugene H. Methvin, "Guess Who Spells Disaster for Education?" *Reader's Digest*, May 1984, p. 91.

6. Larry J. Sabato, *PAC Power: Inside the World of Political Action Committees*, (New York: W. W. Norton, 1984), p. 17.

7. Neill, "NEA: New Powerhouse in the Democratic Party," p. 85.

8. Brian Sullam, "The NEA Discovers the Ballot," *Nation*, April 24, 1976, p. 498.

9. Eugene H. Methvin, "The NEA: A Washington Lobby Run Rampant," *Reader's Digest*, November 1978, p. 99.

10. Letter from Rachelle Horowitz, Director AFT/COPE, to Donna Horton, National Commission on Election Information, Washington, D.C., October 17, 1984.

11. Ibid.

12. Telephone interview with Ray Skuse, Director of Political Affairs, New York State United Teachers, AFL–CIO, Albany, N.Y., June 21, 1985.

13. Ibid.

14. "Power to the Pedagogues," *Time*, July 12, 1976, p. 67.

15. Dale Pullen, *The U.S. Congress Handbook 1986, 99th Congress* (McLean, Va., n.p., 1986).

16. Alan Rosenthal and Susan Fuhrman, *Legislative Education Leadership in the States* (Washington, D.C.: Institute for Educational Leadership, 1981), pp. 28–29.

17. Stanley E. Elam, "Teachers in Politics and the Merger Issue," *Phi Delta Kappan*, October 1976, p. 194.

18. Methvin, "The NEA: A Washington Lobby Run Rampant," p. 97.

19. Ibid., p. 101.

20. Terry Herndon, "Reply to *Reader's Digest*," *Phi Delta Kappan*, February 1979, p. 420.

21. Ibid.

22. Ibid., p. 423.

23. Russell Kirk, "Trouble for the NEA," *National Review*, October 7, 1980, p. 127.

24. Russell Kirk, "The NEA Plans Our Future," *National Review*, November 11, 1976, p. 1301.

25. Ibid.

26. Chester E. Finn, Jr., "Teacher Politics," *Commentary*, February 1983, p. 39.

27. Ibid., p. 29.

28. Ibid.

29. Chapman, "The Teachers' Coup," p. 9.

30. Ibid., p. 11.

31. Stanley E. Elam, "NEA Pressure Politics and the Public Interest," *Phi Delta Kappan*, December 1980, p. 235.

32. Sullam, "The NEA Discovers the Ballot," p. 498.

33. Methvin, "Guess Who Spells Disaster for Education?" p. 93.

34. Elam, "Teachers in Politics and the Merger Issue," p. 194.

35. Samuel L. Blumenfeld, *NEA: Trojan Horse in American Education* (Boise, Idaho: Paradigm, 1984), p. 262.

36. Ibid.

37. Ibid., p. xii.

38. Ibid., p. x.

39. Ibid., p. xii.

40. Ibid.

41. Ibid., p. 139.

42. "Save Our Schools," *Newsletter*, May 1985, p. 7.

43. Ibid., pp. 1–2.

44. Ibid., p. 2.

45. Ibid., p. 4.

46. Ibid., p. 7.

47. Ibid., p. 5.

48. National Education Association, *The Radical Right Attack on the National Education Association* (Washington, D.C., March 1985) p. 1.

49. Ibid., p. 2.

50. Ibid., p. 13.

51. Ibid., p. 1.

52. Ibid.

53. Ibid., p. 10.

54. Ibid.

55. Ibid.

56. "Power of the Pedagogues," p. 67.

57. George H. Gallup, "The 16th Annual Gallop Poll of the Public's Attitudes Toward the Public Schools," *Phi Delta Kappan*, September 1984, p. 35.

58. Ibid., p. 34.

59. Ibid., p. 32.

60. Michael W. Kirst, *Who Controls Our Schools?* (New York: W. H. Freeman, 1984), p. 141.

61. Ibid., p. 142.

62. *New York Times*, July 2, 1985, p. A13.

63. *New York Times*, July 8, 1986, p. C5.

64. Sabato, *PAC Power*, pp. 161–62.

65. Ibid., p. 5.

66. Ibid., pp. 10–11.

67. "Senate Votes to Put Limit on PAC Gifts," *Virginia Ledger-Star*, August 12, 1986, p. A8.

68. Sabato, *PAC Power*, p. 185.

69. "Senate Votes to Put Limit on PAC Gifts," p. A1.

## 2

# The NEA: A Political Giant

Within the past generation, the NEA has emerged as a formidable political giant. Through its lobbying and endorsement of political candidates, the NEA stands as the most influential group in the educational lobby. Still there are problems that face this largest of unions. In legislation, there is often a lack of unity among the members of the educational lobby on both state and national levels. In politics, the NEA may suffer some divisiveness among its members by endorsing specific candidates of a political party.

What has been the political success of NEA? By and large, the NEA has done extremely well in supporting candidates for the U.S. Senate and House. From 1972 through the 1984 election, NEA–PAC (political action committee) endorsed candidates won 76 percent of the elections.[1] In that time they endorsed 2,062 candidates and helped elect 1,573.[2] In 1972, one observer credited the NEA with being responsible for the election of some thirty congressmen, senators and governors.[3] In 1974, NEA–PAC claimed the highest winning percentage among major political action committees. By 1976, NEA had contributed to the election of a president of the United States. In the 1986 congressional election, 80 percent of NEA-backed candidates won.[4] Surely the NEA has been reasonably effective in politics.

The transformation from political naif to political sophisticate was not made without a struggle. When a citizenship committee suggested in 1960 that the NEA accept as a theme for that year, "Every

Teacher a Politician," it was rejected out of hand by the leadership. The reasoning, according to one NEA leader, was that teachers "don't want to be thought of as politicians (because) they are just not interested."[5] More important, teachers wanted to be professionals, and the NEA thought of itself as the organization for professionalism.

By 1986, the NEA was intensely political. One indication of that transformation was the speech given that year at the NEA convention by Steven McAuliffe, the husband of Christa McAuliffe, the first teacher selected to travel in space in the ill-fated *Challenger* spacecraft. In the ceremony honoring the late teacher and NEA member, her husband used the occasion to stress the need for political action. In a speech that "drew sustained applause," McAuliffe spelled out the need for educational politics:

I hope that you will return to your states and use Christa's efforts and her spirit to get involved in the arena effectively to recruit and elect education candidates, to unseat those who support education with their words, but not with their appropriations. And, most of all, that you stay in education at least until we have a system which honors teachers and rewards teachers as they deserve.[6]

This change in political attitudes has been dramatic. In 1956, the NEA Research Division conducted a membership poll asking whether members should participate in politics. Only one fourth said yes.[7] Nearly twenty years later at the 1975 Representative Assembly, the highest policy-making body in the NEA, 92.6 percent of the delegates favored the NEA's endorsement of a Presidential candidate.[8] Even though this latter group was composed of the most active NEA members, it signalled a major shift in attitude.

What had caused the change? There were two reasons for the politicization of the NEA: the rise of teacher unionism in the 1960s and the emergence of the militancy of the civil rights movement, also in the 1960s. Consequently, as NEA affiliates won collective bargaining victories, they also became aware of the potential of political involvement. In 1965, a few short years after the breakthrough bargaining victory by the AFT in New York City, the Utah

NEA affiliate organized the first state political action committee with the purpose of raising funds and supporting political candidates.[9] By 1969, when the NEA national leadership was considering its own national PAC there were already twenty-two state NEA PACs.[10]

Still, the political initiative had come from the NEA leadership on state and national levels. NEA members were still hesitant over "unprofessional" activity. One scholar concluded that until the mid-1970s "many people both in the leadership and the membership of the NEA believed that political participation of the kind proposed by the NEA-PAC was not in the best interests of the NEA."[11]

The example of the militant civil rights movement of the 1960s had an impact on the NEA leadership. The civil rights movement's indirect pressure of picketing, boycotting and marches, coupled with a voter registration drive, sent a clear lesson to interest groups. And that lesson was not lost on the NEA leadership. Between 1969 and 1976, when the NEA endorsed its first presidential candidate, NEA leaders maintained a steady drumbeat for political involvement. NEA presidents such as Helen Bain, George Fischer and John Ryor regularly made statements on the need for teachers to "elect friends of education."[12] The NEA newspaper carried many articles on the need for teachers to get involved in politics.

For the NEA rank and file, the change of attitudes came painfully. NEA members took pride in an association that regarded itself as professional. Indeed, teachers could concentrate on education and learning—rather than on the blue-collar goals of its smaller rival, the AFT. However, concern about such blue-collar goals as salaries and working conditions grew among the teaching profession.

One turning point for the NEA was the 1972 withdrawal of administrators from its ranks. The AFT had scored the NEA as being a company union since it maintained the membership of principals and other management school employees. (Ironically, the AFT would later welcome supervisors to its ranks.) Nevertheless, the die was cast for the NEA in its road to becoming a union. By 1981, the editor of the NEA publication could exclaim that the "NEA is proud to be part of the labor movement."[13] The allusion was partly correct. Although the NEA was now considered a labor organization, it was not affiliated with the AFL-CIO (as was the AFT), and it strongly resisted such a move. Nonetheless, the NEA considered itself "labor."

From being a part of labor, it was just a short step to consider being politically active. The NEA had traditionally maintained lobbying efforts in Congress and in state legislatures, but it had stopped short of endorsing candidates. Again, the NEA had the example of the AFT, where the parent AFL-CIO regularly supported political candidates.

Two developments firmly entrenched the NEA in politics. First was the creation of a national NEA-PAC in 1972. This established the NEA role in politics. Second, and more controversial, was the endorsement by the NEA of a presidential candidate in 1976. This made the NEA highly visible in politics. The creation of a national PAC broke the psychological barrier of "professionalism" in the NEA. The endorsement of Governor Jimmy Carter in 1976 made the NEA a political target for the other side.

Let us examine the record of the NEA in lobbying and in supporting political candidates. We shall concentrate on the operations, impact and criticism made of these efforts.

## LOBBYING

The huge eight-story NEA headquarters building on the corner of 16th and M Streets, in Washington, D.C., is but a half dozen blocks from the White House. This proximity has both a symbolic and real significance. Dale Lestina, former manager of NEA lobbying and now manager of government relations special projects, points out the significance. He recalled that he would walk the six blocks to the White House for early morning breakfast meetings during the administration of Carter, a man the NEA was instrumental in electing.[14] It was the height of NEA power and influence.

On the other hand, these same six blocks could prove to be interminably long. Phone calls to the Reagan White House went unanswered because the NEA had backed Carter twice and opposed Reagan. During the Carter administration, Lestina described the NEA as being on the "offense," whereas during the

Reagan years the NEA has been "on the defensive, just trying to hold our own."[15] Such are the vagaries of politics.

The NEA has maintained a lobbying effort throughout its history. Nevertheless, it has only been in the past decade with concomitant political involvement that these efforts have become highly sophisticated. For example, it has only been since 1981 that legislative efforts by the NEA have become prioritized. In the past, all bills, whether educational or social in nature, received equal emphasis by NEA lobbyists.[16] Moreover, it has only been within recent memory that the NEA has attempted to coalesce other lobbying groups into a united front both on a state and national level.

Some NEA advocates consider the lobbying efforts of the NEA to have been its main strength. Others contend that the NEA, along with other education groups, have failed to present an educational "united front." Allan West, former NEA staff member and historian of the organization, believes that for the NEA "legislative action in the state and national capitols has been the most effective of all activities for the growth and improvement of the nation's public schools and institutions of higher education."[17] On the other hand, Milbrey McLaughlin and James Catterall argue that the NEA, as well as other members of the education lobby on a state level, have been guilty of "internal disarray," and often ineffective.[18]

The operation of the national lobbying arm of the NEA is highly developed. Policy is made by the appropriate democratic constituents of the NEA and carried out by the headquarters staff. The headquarters staff is comprised of six full-time lobbyists. Each lobbyist is a specialist in one of six areas, ranging from money issues to social issues. This specialist will spearhead the campaign on his special issue, and the other lobbyists provide aid as the needs of the legislative program require.

Policy is made by the Representative Assembly, a group composed of elected delegates from every state that meets in convention each summer. One method for gathering ideas for policy issues is from hearings across the country with NEA members. These hearings are conducted by a special legislative committee appointed by the NEA president, numbering nine NEA members from state affiliates. This information is forwarded to the president, who reports to the Executive Committee made up of national officials. In turn, the officials report to the Board of Directors, the highest administrative body, composed of some 126 NEA members elected by state affiliates on a proportional ratio basis. Finally, the program is presented to the Representative Assembly, composed of 7,500 state and local delegates, for ratification. Another method of gathering policy ideas is for state affiliates to forward issues to the annual meeting of the Representative Assembly.

The making of NEA legislative policy reflects the decentralized nature of the organization. Concomitantly, this loose structure parallels an educational system in the United States that has a state focus. Until 1986, NEA presidents were elected for a maximum of two-year terms, for a total of four years. Now they are able to serve for six years. This system has hampered the organization in effectiveness and forced the chief executive officer, who is hired by the officials, to provide the continuity. Indeed, under Terry Herndon, former Executive Director of the NEA 1973 to 1983, the organization seemed to have distinctive style.

On the other hand, the AFT has had the same president, Albert Shanker, since 1974. This has enabled Shanker to project a constant image as a spokesman for education, despite the smaller size of his union. Even NEA officials concede that the limited nature of the NEA presidency has enabled the AFT to gain an upper hand, especially in projecting a strong media image.[19]

Still, the thrust of the NEA in policy terms has been to promote a stronger federal commitment to education. Two of its goals throughout the past decades has been for greater federal financial involvement and for the creation of a U.S. Department of Education with cabinet rank. In turn, this goal has led to increasing efforts by the national NEA office to exert a stronger influence among its ranks. Some NEA members have criticized this growing national NEA trend. Two former Directors of State Affiliates have claimed that there has been a "shift in the balance of power within the NEA" toward the national staff.[20] Indeed, Bill Boyton and John Lloyd, these two NEA state directors, charged in 1984 that the endorsement of Walter Mondale for president by the NEA was the result of a ploy by the national staff.[21]

Policy is grouped according to a three-tier system under the new, prioritized legislative system. This grouping mainly separates educational and social issues, and gives precedence to certain educational objectives. In the 1986 legislative program, Tier One goals were to increase federal funding and recognition of collective bargaining rights for teachers.[22] These objectives have remained relatively the same since 1970, although at that time a specific percentage of one-third was the goal for federal assumption of educational costs. Also, in 1970 the creation of a Department of Education was high on the NEA list—a goal that was finally realized.

Of the fourteen items in the NEA legislative program on a Tier Two level, all but three concern education. These include such items as the opposition to tuition tax credits, vouchers and the abolition of the Department of Education. The three social issues affect civil rights, social security and taxation.[23]

Tier One and Tier Two policies are usually legislative bills that originate with the NEA and are introduced by friendly senators and congressmen. On the other hand Tier Three priorities are mainly bills monitored by NEA lobbyists. These may include some educational matters such as adult education but usually are issues of larger social policy. Some of these in the 1986 NEA legislative program included retirement, wage-price controls, immigration and health policy—in short, issues only indirectly affecting the welfare of teachers.

How successful has the NEA been in pursuing its legislative agenda? Both on a state and national level, the NEA has achieved substantial success. Two national victories in the past two decades illustrate NEA power and influence: the passage of a federal aid to education law in 1965, and the creation of a Department of Education in 1980. In both cases the NEA played a crucial role.

The passage of the Elementary and Secondary Education Act (ESEA) in 1965 by the U.S. Congress was a breakthrough in education. For the first time in more than a hundred years of attempts, federal aid to public schools became a reality. It was a triumph for the education lobby over strong odds, but most of all for the NEA, which was the chief proponent for federal aid. Robert E. McKay, chief NEA lobbyist, glowed over the NEA role:

At the risk of sounding terribly immodest, I have concluded that the NEA was responsible for the passage of ESEA. Not solely responsible—but without the action and the leadership of the National Education Association, I am sure the bill would not have passed. . . . I can't say enough for the exceptionally skillful and effective work done by members of the NEA legislative staff.[24]

McKay may have exaggerated but not by much. Historians associate the coalition politics engendered by the leadership of President Lyndon Johnson, a former Senate Majority Leader and able negotiator, with an overwhelmingly Democratic Senate and House. Opposition to federal aid came mostly from Catholic educators who wanted some aid to parochial schools, and Southern educators who were wary of dismantling segregated schools. A compromise was made whereby some minor benefits would accrue to parochial schools without violating the constitutional wall separating church and state. Meanwhile, the civil rights movement was in full flourish by 1965, making the continuance of de jure segregated schools in the South no longer tenable. Nonetheless, it was the steady and insistent drumbeat of the NEA that accounted for the chief support to federal aid. Understandably, the NEA would want to enlarge the federal role and soon after made increased federal funding a priority issue.

Another great victory for the NEA was the creation of a Department of Education. This was a particularly sweet success since strong opposition to such an idea came from within the NEA's own political constituency: liberal, labor and civil rights groups. But the NEA had made the department a major issue in the 1970s and tied it to its presidential endorsement in 1976. Consequently, with President Carter's support, the idea had major backing. But it was the assiduous work of the NEA lobbyists that pulled the bill through. It was an extremely narrow victory. The vote cleared the Government Operations committee by one vote. A diversionary attack by opponents raised non-tangential issues such as abortion, busing and school prayer. The bill squeaked through by a four-vote margin in the House. The NEA had managed a narrow victory. Now even former opponents of the Department of Education, such as Albert Shanker, according to NEA lobbyists, are reluctant to see it abolished.[25]

NEA lobbyists are perceived by congressmen and senators dealing with education as "professional" and people of "integrity." Some of the senators and congressional staff sampled, found the NEA lobbyists to have "the greater influence" in Congress of any of the representatives from the education lobby.[26] They also noted no contact with AFT lobbyists save through printed materials. For example, Michael Hill, legislative director for Congressman Dave Kildee, Democrat of Michigan and a former teacher and AFT member, considers the NEA as "the stronger presence in education."[27] He cites the "good work in researching legal matters that is absolutely trustworthy of NEA lobbyists" and is unmatched by any other lobbying group "either in education or any other lobby."[28] Congressman Kildee, he states, is ideologically close to the NEA educational philosophy. Amy Shulz, legislative assistant to Senator Quentin Burdick, Democrat of North Dakota, echoed these sentiments. Senator Burdick tends to "a similar philosophy" to the NEA, and his aide finds the NEA lobbyists "well informed, knowing the issues and with a good political sense."[29] His Republican colleague, Senator Mark Andrews also has respect for the NEA. His legislative aide Deanna Marlowe considers NEA lobbyists to be "fairly effective."[30] But it was Congressman Jack Brooks, Democrat of Texas, and his administrative assistant Sharon Matts who consider the NEA lobbyists to be most effective during the drive for a Department of Education. The NEA was not only highly able on a national level, according to Matts, but brought in NEA members to the home state offices of congressmen to petition for the Department of Education.[31]

In 1976, the NEA formed a grass roots corps of volunteers to personally contact legislators both at home and in Washington. According to John Conway, the Congressional Contact Team Coordinator, the NEA seeks to "broaden the political involvement of members."[32] Originally two members from each legislator's congressional district were recruited for the team. Since that time, the NEA recruits from five to eight volunteers.[33] Conway has a list of some 1,100 contact team volunteers.[34] The contact teams visit their own legislators in Washington to advocate the NEA position. And the contact team from each district visits the lawmaker in their home district. This personal touch never fails to impress lawmakers.

This sophistication extends to the state level. In Virginia, for example, the Virginia Education Association, operates a grass roots supplement to aid state education lobbyists. There are teacher contacts for every legislator, teachers in every school to organize mailings on an issue and teachers trained as lobbyists. Teachers from the home districts bring pressure to bear on their own legislators. According to NEA lobbyist Roland Dorfer, "the most effective pressure is an articulate teacher's personal contact with his or her legislator."[35]

Despite the active lobbying, the NEA has been eclipsed as a high-spending Washington lobbyist. In 1959, the NEA was listed as the highest spending of the professional associations. Since 1969, however, the NEA has not been included among the twenty-four spenders.[36] Still, the NEA spends a considerable sum on lobbying activities nationally; some $800,000 to $900,000 in 1985.[37] Since education remains largely a state function, the focus of NEA lobbying efforts have to be on that level.

### Coalition Politics

The strongest criticism of the education lobby, in which the NEA is the major player, is that it lacks unity in pressing for educational legislation. This has been true, according to some critics, both on a national and state level. Some scholars have considered the state education lobby to be in "internal disarray," when in a time of retrenchment, rivalries are seriously counterproductive.[38] According to these critics, the problem is that groups within the education lobby "pursue their own objective," thus "damaging education's position."[39] One state legislator believes that the education lobby will never be able to coalesce because of the divergent self-interests of each group.[40]

On a national level that problem seems to have abated. The education lobby, after a period of confusion, united on the issue that proved a common denominator—funding. The NEA's Dale Lestina believes that the education lobby "learned to coalesce on funding issues."[41] Former Senator Mark Andrews (R-N.D.) believes that "by and large the education lobby has been cohesive on funding issues."[42] This is the result of the newly formed Committee for Education Funding. The committee is comprised of representatives from the NEA, AFT, American Association of School Administrators, Elementary Principals Association, Secondary Principals Association, National Association of Boards of Education, National Parents and Teachers Association, American Vocational Associa-

tion, and Great City Schools Council—in short, the entire education lobby.

On the other hand, issues not pertaining to school funding vary
according to the self-interests of the lobbying organizations. School
boards may not want the same legislation affecting education that
do school teachers. Lestina admits that the members of the education lobby pursue separate agendas, for the most part, to achieve
their interests.[43]

There have been instances when the NEA has exerted strong
leadership on a state level. In California, where the NEA staff is
over 200, the California Teachers Association (CTA) was a preem-
inent leader in the education lobby. According to students of California educational politics, the CTA "was considered the most
powerful professional interest group in the state."[44] Oscar Anderson, the chief CTA lobbyist, was perceived as "more than just a
special interest group representative; he was a leading spokesman
for the education community on finance matters and the major source
of expert advice outside the State Department of Education for
legislation."[45] Let us pursue the California case more closely.


### Case Study

An examination of coalition politics in California, an uncom-
monly education-minded state with high expenditures for public
schooling, reveals the transformation of the education lobby from
disarray to coalition politics. In their study of the impact of the
*Serrano* decision on education in California, Richard F. Elmore
and Milbrey W. McLaughlin document this change in the early to
late 1970s. The CTA, once the most powerful interest group in
education in the state, had "to play smart coalition politics to achieve
its objectives" as the education lobby confronted the *Serrano* decision.[46]

The *Serrano* decision became a landmark case in school finance.
John Serrano, social worker, petitioned the California courts to redress the financial inequities in a school finance system based on
the property tax. This system created stringent inequities. Wealthy
areas raise more money for schools than do districts with less valuable property. This disparity is true both within states and among
states. For example, property rich Fairfax County Virginia, a sub-

urb of Washington, D.C., raises more money for schools than does
the county of Accomac, which is composed of poor farmland. And
among states, California far overspends Mississippi in funding public education. This problem of financial inequity has yet to be sat-
isfactorily resolved.

In 1971, the California Supreme Court ruled in favor of Serrano.
School financing plans based on property wealth were not constitutional. The *Serrano* decision spurred school finance reformers in
California to press the legislature to restructure the school finance
system. In that fashion, a parent need not have to move to a more
affluent district to obtain better schools.

The *Serrano* decision was a simple solution to a complex issue.
The task was to translate this decision into an effective piece of
legislation. Politics, including educational politics, in this country
more often than not means compromise, despite praiseworthy objectives. There are many constituencies with competing interests
to consider. Such was the case in California.

Two attempts were made by school finance reformers to implement the *Serrano* decision in California. Both were initially perceived as successful, but later adjudged failures. Both incorporated
some measure of equalization, yet the first was criticized by some
school finance reformers as "dishonest" and the second "a gigantic
fraud."[47] In the end, Proposition 13—a grass roots referendum to
cut property taxes—would render the attempts at school finance
reform moot. The politics of retrenchment made school finance
reform a luxury.

The first attempt to implement a Serrano legislative solution followed shortly after the court's decision in 1972. The prospects for
some degree of equalization seemed good. The political actors appeared willing to give finance reform a chance. A newly elected
State Superintendent of Public Instruction was a black liberal reformer—Wilson Riles. Moreover, the California legislature had a
history of actively pursuing school change. Most elements of the
education lobby were amenable to finance reform. Even the conservative Republican governor, Ronald Reagan, appeared willing
to compromise on the issue in order to achieve his goal of property
tax relief. It was a hopeful scenario that went awry, partly because
of the lack of cohesion among the members of the education lobby.

After false starts, Reagan was able to reach a compromise plan with the Democratic Assembly leader, Robert Moretti. Four main issues were agreed upon: (1) the need to provide property tax relief—a Reagan goal; (2) the need for money for schools—a goal of the education lobby; (3) the need for some equalization formula to implement Serrano—a goal of the finance reformers; and (4) the need to find a mechanism to pay for it all.

The Reagan-Moretti plan was submitted to the Senate as Senate Bill 90. It failed to pass in its first attempt, indicating the confused support of the education lobby. In the following state legislative elections, Reagan sought to elect members of the legislature that would support SB90. The CTA joined forces to campaign against the enemies of SB90. In the next session SB90 was passed. The bill provided more money for schools but weak equalization strategies. Supporters termed the effort a "strategic masterpiece" since side payments were made to various members of the education lobby, whereas school finance reformers considered the bill "a dishonest covenant, secretly arrived at."[48]

In time even the members of the education lobby came to realize that SB90 was an "inferior strategy" that produced a "fiscal Frankenstein."[49] One fallout was an unnecessary sales tax that created excessive surpluses. The education lobby became disconcerted by its weak rubber stamp role. CTA lobbyist Jim Donnaly expressed the sentiments of the group by declaring that "we did not believe that we could have gotten more."[50] Governor Reagan had blunted the thrust of the education lobby with side payments to various groups to obtain wide support. One education lobbyist termed SB90 a watershed. The education lobby felt that SB90, in the end, hurt education and "that realization is what drew the education coalition together and was the birth of coalition politics in California education."[51]

The second attempt to implement Serrano was another matter. The education lobby learned to unite and played a stronger, more positive role. The second attempt took place in 1975 with another national and state scenario. The nation was in the throes of "stagflation"—high inflation coupled with high unemployment. There was a new governor—a centrist liberal, Jerry Brown, whom the CTA had vigorously supported.

The education lobby did not come together without false starts. Governor Brown had rejected a bill that would have substantially raised teacher salaries. The CTA, fresh from its support of Brown, was angered, and union officials "accused Brown of a breach of promise to education in the state."[52] Some members of the education lobby, such as the California School Boards Association, had supported Brown on the issue. Again there was "disarray among the educational interest groups."[53]

Finally, the education lobby united. Members banded together in the Tuesday Night Group (so named because that was when they met) under the initiative of Ron Prescott, a lobbyist for the Los Angeles School System. Other members of the group included representatives from the CTA, the California Federation of Teachers, the United Teachers of Los Angeles (merged union), the California School Boards Association, the Association of California School Administrators and the five urban school districts. In the words of one lobbyist: "All of us were doing our own thing until we discovered we could all lose."[54]

Success came as a result. In 1977, Assembly Bill 65 was passed with the required two-thirds majority. The bill provided for greater Serrano equalization concessions through a complicated power equalization formula advocated by school finance reformers. The education lobby had worked hard for passage and mobilized 600 teachers, administrators and school board members to march on Sacramento, the state capitol. Still, some school finance reformers wanted greater equalization and labeled AB65 "a gigantic fraud on California taxpayers."[55]

There were lessons to be learned from the Serrano experience. First, educational politics demanded a united education lobby. Second, the process of compromise and negotiation among several interest groups hinders large-scale reform in education. And third, the politics of retrenchment, brought on by Proposition 13 and followed by attempts to balance state budgets, impelled the education lobby to widen its coalition with other social agencies to obtain more support.

## POLITICAL ACTION

Beyond lobbying there is the larger world of endorsing and supporting specific political candidates in hopes of securing desired legislation and governmental policy. That is where controversy begins.

The NEA crossed the psychological barrier from exclusively professional association to a politicalized union in the 1960s. The NEA leadership, as well as some teachers, foresaw the need to involve the organization in politics even to the highest level of the White House, where legislation could be vetoed by the president.

However, it was not the national leadership of the NEA that was first to become politically involved. Utah had the first state political action committee in 1965 endorsing and supporting state candidates. By 1969, twenty-two states had political action committees.[56] The national leadership followed in 1968 with an exploratory program called Teachers in Politics. This resulted in a Task Force to consider a national political action committee. By 1972, the National NEA-PAC was established and endorsing national candidates, and by 1975, the NEA would endorse presidential candidates.

Ironically, the resistance to a national PAC came from the state affiliates. State affiliates were concerned that their own PACs might suffer from the national NEA-PAC. The national leadership was able to quell such fears. The leaders' strong suit was the argument that a political action arm was essential on a national basis and state PACs would have a large policy role. With the approval of the Representative Assembly, the large group of NEA delegates that make policy, the NEA first endorsed candidates nationally in 1972. There was, however, no authorization to endorse a presidential candidate, and the best the national leadership could do was refuse to support President Richard Nixon for re-election on the grounds that he lacked interest in education.[57]

By 1980 the NEA-PAC politics was a regular NEA issue. NEA President Willard McGuire would comment in *Today's Education*, the NEA newspaper, that "if we teachers have to become politicians . . . we will do so."[58] That issue of the newspaper was largely devoted to politics. Primaries in four states, geographically selected to present a national focus, were examined: New Hampshire, Florida, Indiana and California—representing the Northeast, South, Midwest and Far West.

In New Hampshire, teachers were able to obtain over 3,500 signatures of registered Democrats for President Carter. In Florida,

NEA members gained sixty-three seats in the Democratic caucus. In Indiana, NEA members were attempting to best the 1976 mark of twenty teachers selected as delegates to the national conventions. In California, NEA teachers attempted to carry a Congressional candidate into office after a narrow 1978 loss of only 540 votes.[59]

The NEA-PAC now endorses candidates chosen by a steering committee with a great deal of input from state affiliates. Indeed, a majority of members of the steering committee are chosen from state affiliates. One member from each state, chosen by the state PACs, belongs to the national NEA-PAC. In addition, the following serve as members of NEA-PAC: the NEA President and six National Board members; three Executive Committee members; five minority representatives from the Black, Spanish-speaking, Indian, Oriental and Women's caucuses; one retired teacher; and two members of the NEA Student Program.

The procedures for endorsing a president were finalized in 1974. The NEA Representative Assembly, polled on the issue, responded overwhelmingly by a 92.6 percent favorable vote to support a presidential candidate.[60]

### Political Training Program

The NEA conducts an elaborate and sophisticated training program for politically inclined members within its ranks. The purpose is to achieve NEA legislative objectives through lobbying or supporting endorsed political candidates. More than 100,000 of such political activists have been trained. They average some 150 or more activists per targeted political campaign.[61]

The program consists of a two-and-one-half-hour workshop guided by ten highly developed booklets covering the political spectrum. Among these topics are some sophisticated techniques, such as conducting opinion polls and targeting strategies for endorsed candidates. Each workshop is divided into three broad areas, and is limited to some 25-30 participants.

The areas and the ten booklets are: Group One, *You and Politics*, a rationale for becoming politically involved; Group Two, *How To Set Up and Operate a Local Association Political Action Pro-*

*gram, How To Raise Money for NEA-PACs Education Defense Fund, How To Endorse Candidates, How To Recruit, Organize and Manage Volunteers,* and *How To Run Voter Contact Programs.* These are the staples of political campaigning. Group Three consists of strategies that go beyond regular support: *How To Conduct Opinion Polls, How To Target Elections, How To Participate in Party Politics,* and *How To Prepare and Use Print Communications.*

The aim of the training workshop is fourfold. First, the NEA hopes to realize its legislative program. Second, the NEA seeks a role as leader in the politics of education rather than "being forced to react."[62] Third, the NEA seeks to obtain the most for its resources, both human and financial. And, finally, the NEA wants to "head off other special interest groups with competing interests and conflicting needs."[63] NEA members are instructed that "the most effective way in which the association can achieve significant gains for members and for public education is through political organizing."[64] This would seem to place collective bargaining as secondary.

The first part of the workshop deals with the reason for the NEA and its members to become politically involved. This section stresses among other things the growing influence of the NEA politically and the concommitant threat of the "Radical Right." The idea that public education is by its very nature political and requires political involvement is proclaimed. Moreover, teachers enjoy a certain measure of political esteem and credibility. According to the training booklet, a 1984 *USA Today* poll indicated that 45 percent of the electorate would support a candidate endorsed by the NEA. This was the highest percentage of groups such as farmers and environmental organizations. Liberal groups that scored low on the survey included the National Organization of Women, with 22 percent, and the National Association for the Advancement of Colored People (NAACP), with 20 percent of the vote. Conservative groups that scored low included the Moral Majority, with 18 percent of the vote.[65] The appeal of teachers in politics seems clear.

Another reason for political involvement cited by the NEA is the threat of the Radical Right and its PACs. According to the NEA, the top four PACs are those of the Radical Right having more than

$30 million combined in contributions, which dwarfs the NEA's $2.5 million. Still, the NEA is the top labor PAC and is the twelfth largest in contributions.[66]

The workshop devotes fifty minutes of the two-and-one-half-hour session to how NEA members can influence others, through various means for political decisions.[67] Included in each of the ten booklets are opinion surveys to provide feedback to the NEA on how members perceived the quality of instruction and materials.

The second part of the workshop deals with the basic operations of a political campaign. The five booklets in this group deal with creating a local PAC, raising money for such PACs, endorsing candidates, using campaign volunteers and running voter contact programs.

The first booklet in this group sets the guidelines for the formation of a PAC. The task of this PAC is then outlined as raising funds, recruiting volunteers and endorsing candidates. Two of the more interesting suggestions in the booklet are to form coalitions "to create the broadest base for endorsed candidates" and for the NEA members to participate in party politics.[68]

The booklet on fund raising has specific tips for NEA activists. Simple suggestions, such as telling members success stories of NEA PACs and soliciting members and the reminder to "ask and ask again," are included.[69] The rationale for fund raising is the NEA struggle in education over such issues as tuition tax credits and merit pay and social issues such as "the threat of the "Radical Right" and the "Moral Majority.""[70]

Endorsement procedures are elaborate. Political candidates are given thorough questionnaires on issues; moreover, they are subject to intense scrutiny through interviews. All candidates seeking the endorsement of the NEA must undergo this procedure, with one exception. That exception is for incumbent members of Congress who have been *previously* endorsed by the NEA and who have a minimum 80 percent voting record in the previous Congress on NEA issues.

In addition, there are guidelines in the allocation of resources for the various political campaigns. Priority is given to allocating resources to races that have been very close with a pro-education incumbent; by "close" is meant a race where a candidate was elected by a margin of 56 percent or less.[71] The second priority is to defeat an anti-education incumbent, again with a similar marginal vote differential in the previous election. And the third priority is to commit resources in a contest with an open seat (where incumbent is not running for reelection) with a marginal election with a pro-education candidate. There are four other categories of priorities in descending order, following the same logic as the first three.

The endorsement process is spelled out in an endorsement kit provided state affiliates. These include a questionnaire, procedures for the composition of interview teams, and guidelines for the interviews. The interview team consists of a chair, a host, a reporter and a tracker, a congressional contact team representative and the PAC chairman or a Representative of UniServ, the NEA staff. The chair conducts the interview, the reporter listens "and observes facial expressions and body language," and the tracker "steers the conversation back on track if it goes astray."[72] The interview process is standard and resembles the guidelines of a standard research text.

Perhaps the most important part of the training series deals with volunteers. The NEA perceives volunteers to be its basic campaign tool. There are only two types of politics practiced in this era of campaigning: media politics, and grass roots politics involving volunteers. The NEA eschews the first and promotes the grass roots variety, whose "impact comes from people—NEA members carrying out the grass roots tasks necessary to win."[73] The NEA notes that the profile of a typical volunteer resembles that of the NEA member: that is, a person with good income and education. *New York Times* labor reporter A. H. Raskin adds that teacher volunteers possess two "secret" political weapons: namely, that teachers are enthusiastic campaign workers and that they bring prestige to the political campaign.[74]

The NEA booklet on volunteers covers the gamut of managing NEA members who volunteer for political activity. This includes considering the psychology of those who volunteer, recruiting volunteers and organizing a volunteer campaign. According to the NEA, people volunteer in political campaigns for three main reasons: for social needs, for diversion, and, most important, for a belief. A volunteer must be given a clear job to do, a good reason for doing it and the tools to get it done. Some of these jobs are as follows: voter registration drives, telephoning, distributing literature, polling, canvassing door-to-door, soliciting signatures for petitions, mailing, administrative tasks, research, targeting and getting out the vote. In short, everything that is involved in a political campaign.

In conjunction with the volunteer program, the NEA has coupled a section on voter contact. There are four ways to get in touch with voters. First is the mass media, which the NEA does not pursue. The other three ways involve volunteers: by phone, mail or in person. Such contact enables NEA activists to persuade nonvoting members to vote and solicit funds for the NEA PACs, and recruit other volunteers and poll members. It should be stressed that the political contact by NEA volunteers is mainly aimed at their own NEA membership to support candidates that would seek the legislative goals of the organization.

The three methods of personal contact are meticulously discussed in the NEA manual. A specific method of giving telephone contact is presented. Tips on direct mail campaigns are suggested. This may involve delivering a pro- or anti-candidate message, raising money, getting out the vote or sustaining the corps of volunteers. Sample mailings are presented. Little is left to the imagination.

Similarly, in discussing the third and most effective method, person-to-person contact, a ritual is presented. NEA volunteers are programmed to make this "the most powerful form of voter contact."[75] The NEA member must follow five steps in personal contact. First, the volunteer introduces himself/herself to the NEA member as representing the NEA. Second, the "pitch" is given, making the NEA's position clear. Third, the volunteer gives the NEA endorsement of the specific candidate, urging the NEA member to support such NEA endorsed candidates. Fourth, the volunteer repeats the "pitch." Fifth, the volunteer answers specific questions concerning the endorsed candidate. A how-to kit is distributed to NEA volunteers making person-to-person contacts. Finally, each response by the solicited member is coded by the volunteer for future reference.

The third—and final—grouping of NEA material consists of sophisticated techniques not normally required of campaign volunteers. These strategies would usually be performed by professional pollsters or political consultants. They involve conducting survey

research, "targeting" voting groups and using print media. Consequently, the well-trained NEA volunteer can provide services to
an endorsed candidate that might not be available to him or her
because of limited funds.

The manual on survey research is a clear and concise distillation
of opinion polling methods. A simplified form of random sampling
is used, a form that is easy to conduct by the NEA volunteer yet
gives good results in terms of controlling for bias. This method is
systematic sampling, which requires a pollster to choose a se-
quence, say every tenth name, to be polled. Then the volunteer is
instructed on the proper manner in which to compose questionnaires, a crucial aspect of survey research. In this sample, what is
employed is a Likert scale giving gradations of opinion from a negative to positive on a numerical scale. Items on the questionnaire
are correlated with demographic data. Similar procedures are given
on the proper manner in which to conduct interviews of NEA
members. Finally, the manual instructs the volunteer on how to
tabulate the results of the poll and analyze them properly.

The NEA makes a distinction between regular polls and campaign polls. Polls normally indicate who is leading in a political
race. On the other hand, the type of campaign poll conducted by
the NEA volunteer is more in-depth. The NEA manual explains
the difference:

Campaign polls are interested, of course, in who's leading but they care
far more about how voters see the candidates, what they know about them,
the qualities they perceive in them, how they rate their performance, the
intensity of their support or opposition, the issues most important to them,
how they feel about a wide variety of topics.[76]

Another complex strategy taught to NEA volunteers is "targeting." This entails identifying key constitutent groups, such as people who vote and those who don't, and where these groups may
be located within the election district. Key groups would be opinion leaders, labor union members, racial or ethnic groups and se-
nior citizens. Targeting enables the candidate to concentrate on
issues amenable to the particular group. The NEA manual provides mathematical formulas to measure the size of the targeted

group vote, the performance of that group and the degree of independence of the targeted group.

Techniques for print communications are the last of the sophisticated instructions of the NEA volunteer. The NEA manual provides a sound but brief summary of journalistic methods. The aim is to produce print media that will persuade voters. The manual gives important tips on the preparation of print materials. The message must be able to be scanned in twelve seconds—the time research has shown that the ordinary viewer gives to campaign materials. The publications may be posted, mailed or delivered in person. These materials, the manual suggests, may be of wide variety. They include leaflets, brochures, tabloids, letters and booklets. Samples are given.

Finally, the NEA volunteer is urged to participate himself or herself in the political process—either as a party delegate or functionary or as a candidate. The last manual in the series succinctly outlines how the parties work from the precinct to national convention level. A model precinct campaign is presented. As incentive, success stories are told of NEA members in both parties throughout the country. In a final statement, the NEA boasts that "no organization has a membership better suited to gaining influence within the political parties."[77]

In short, the NEA training program and accompanying materials are highly sophisticated. Together, these give the NEA volunteer basic campaign techniques and beyond. In that fashion, the NEA can be reasonably effective in campaign politics.

## FRAGMENTING TEACHER UNITY

What effect does partisan political involvement have on the membership? A crucial issue is the possible divisiveness teacher politics may incur. Partisan politics may alienate members from their teacher unions. Indeed, as Paul Starr has demonstrated in his study of the medical profession, *The Social Transformation of American Medicine*, one of the most difficult problems doctors had in stabilizing the profession was competition among doctors in the nineteenth century. Once the American Medical Association prevailed in eliminating competition among doctors, the profession became united. Today, doctors refrain from competing for clients and indeed refer clients to specialists. The legal profession also frowns on competition among lawyers, and even though there has been some advertising recently of the services of particular law firms, that has been minimal. Similarly, teachers have been relatively united, for the most part, since mass organization began in the 1960s. It remains to be seen, however, whether political involvement may work as a detriment to teacher unity in the future.

There exists conflicting evidence on the divisive effect of teacher politics. On the one hand, the endorsement of Jimmy Carter in 1976 by the NEA may have triggered some negative reactions. That year NEA membership had reached a high of 1,886,532. After entering into politics on a national scale, the NEA lost some 250,000 members by 1983.[78] Moreover, some exit polls in the 1980 election indicated that most teachers voted for Ronald Reagan rather than Carter.[79] And although NEA membership in 1984 comprised 41 percent registered Democrats and 28 percent registered Republicans, NEA polls indicate that union members appeared rather evenly divided on their presidential choices.[80] In 1980, 44 percent voted for Carter and 41 percent voted for Reagan with 15 percent choosing independent candidate John Anderson.[81] In 1984, 56 percent of the NEA membership voted for Mondale while 44 percent chose Reagan.[82] NEA political analysts point out, however, that the percentage vote of NEA members for Mondale was approximately the same as the national percentage for Reagan. Nevertheless, these figures suggest that the membership may be divided on the support of past Democratic candidates endorsed by the NEA.

In addition, fluctuation of contributions to the NEA-PAC suggests a backlash. In 1976, after reaching a total of $681,630 in voluntary contributions for political action, contributions dropped to half that number after the NEA endorsed Carter in 1976.[83] That figure remained the same at some $300,000 until 1982. Complicating the picture was a legal challenge in some sixteen states over the manner of check-off procedures for NEA members to contribute to the political fund. The courts did not resolve the issue until 1978. Nevertheless, political contributions did not increase until some four years later. This shows some disillusionment with NEA politics.

On the other hand, other evidence suggests that teacher union members are less aroused by teacher union politics. There does not appear to be any significant dissent on political policies in the AFT. And, in addition to the NEA poll on political preferences which indicates that most members were Democrats (AFT has no such polls), a Gallup Poll among randomly selected teachers seemed to corroborate those preferences. In October 1984, a month before the presidential election, Gallup showed that most teachers believed former Vice President Mondale to be more likely to improve education. Forty-two percent of those polled thought Mondale would be better for education, whereas 25 percent thought President Reagan would be, and 33 percent either had no opinion or felt that there was little difference on education between the two candidates.[84] Moreover, NEA-PAC contributions ballooned to $2,177,756 in 1984 a figure that was interpreted by NEA political analysts as confirming the organization's political role.[85]

Equally important is the drift of the NEA to the Democratic party. That movement has been equally pronounced in the AFT. As part of the AFL-CIO, which has traditionally supported Democratic party candidates, the AFT has long preferred Democrats on a national level. However, the AFT has been more flexible in state and local politics. In New York, for example, the only state not controlled by the NEA, the AFT has been evenly divided in their support of Republicans and Democrats.[86] And although the AFT backed Mondale, in 1984, there was concern when AFT President Albert Shanker invited President Reagan to speak at the AFT national convention.

The NEA has promoted almost solely Democratic party candidates nationally. In 1984, the NEA supported twenty-six candidates for the United States Senate, none of whom were Republicans, and 304 candidates for the House of Representatives, only 16 of whom were Republicans.[87] The AFT has found itself in a similar bind of being linked almost exclusively with the national Democratic party. In addition to supporting the Democratic presidential ticket in 1984, AFT endorsed 14 candidates for the Senate, all of whom were Democrats, and 134 candidates for the House, only two of whom were Republicans.[88]

According to NEA analysts, few Republicans promoted educational and social legislation in the 97th Congress. These analysts suggest that President Reagan's pressure on some moderate Republicans, who were in the past educationally minded, cost them

NEA support. The teacher organizations have been forced to endorse Democratic candidates on a national level because of the strong educational and ideological split that has developed with the ascent of Ronald Reagan. Conservative Republicans tend to favor private rather than pubic schooling and have sought either tuition tax credits or vouchers that would tend to make private schools flourish while public schools would be shunted aside.

There has been some concern among the teacher unions about the gradual realignment of parties. The Democratic party speaks for minorities—black, feminist and Hispanic—whereas the majoritarian white middle class votes Republican. One Democratic political analyst noted that no Democratic presidential candidate had won a majority of the white middle class since 1948, except Lyndon Johnson.[89] NEA officials aware of this realignment make rhetorical overtones to a "bi-partisan role and emphasizing that [sic] more than ever."[90]

AFT officials are also worried over changing party allegiances. In a memorandum to the AFT Executive Council and liasions for the Committee on Political Education, COPE Director Rachelle Horowitz indicated that she had "been brooding about the results of the 1984 election" and the "steady decline from the days of the formation of the New Deal coalition."[91] Horowitz mused about the possibility of "shifting party loyalties" and concluded that although "a sizable number of Democrats voted for Reagan in 1984 . . . it remains to be seen whether they will embrace the Republican Party as their own."[92]

Nevertheless, AFL-CIO exit polls did not show large-scale defections. According to these polls, members of AFL-CIO unions supported the Democratic presidential candidate by 61–39 percent.[93] Moreover, 72 percent of these members voted for Democrats in the Senate, and 69 percent voted for Democrats in the House.[94] AFL-CIO President Lane Kirkland optimistically concluded that "in the face of an overwhelming landslide for Reagan, our members held firm."[95] Democratic defections came in the non-union South, where only 37 percent of white Southern Democrats voted for Mondale.[96]

For the most part, the teacher unions have followed the lead of the labor movement. They have heeded AFL President Samuel Gompers' historic dictum to reward friends and punish enemies.

There has been little evidence that these labor unions have suffered permanent membership loss because of the political preferences of the union leadership. Union members often separate their
work life from their political preferences and may not vote on single issues. As one NEA member critical of the NEA's endorsement
of Mondale pointed out, "no intelligent voter votes for a President
on his education record alone."[97]

## NOTES

1. National Education Association, *You and Politics: A Workbook Introduction* (Trainer's Guide), Washington, D.C., March 1985, p. 11.

2. Ibid.

3. Constance Trisler Shotts, "The Origin and Development of the National Education Association Political Action Committee, 1969–1976" (Ann
Arbor, Mich.: Xerox University Microfilms, 1976), p. 5.

4. Telephone interview with Joseph Standa, Political Affairs Specialist,
National Education Association, Washington, D.C., November 14, 1986.

5. Willard McGuire, "Politics 1980," *NEA Today*, February–March
1980, p. 26.

6. *New York Times*, July 7, 1986, p. B8.

7. Shotts, "The Origin and Development of the National Education
Association Political Action Committee, 1969–1976," p. 1.

8. Ibid., p. 83.

9. Ibid., p. 3.

10. Ibid., p. 27.

11. Ibid., p. 89.

12. Ibid., p. 14.

13. Willard McGuire, "Labor as a National Movement," *Today's Education*, September 1981, p. 8.

14. Interview with Dale Lestina, Government Relations Specialist, National Education Association, Washington, D.C., June 16, 1986.

15. Ibid.

16. Ibid.

17. Allan M. West, *The National Education Association: The Power Base
for Education* (New York: The Free Press, 1980), p. 162.

18. Milbrey W. McLaughlin and James Catterall, "Notes on the New
Politics of Education," *Education and Urban Society*, May 1984, p. 377.

19. Interview with Dale Lestina.

20. Bill Boyton and John Lloyd, "Why the Largest Teachers Union Puts
Its Staff First and Education Second," *Washington Monthly*, May 1985,
p. 28.

21. Ibid., p. 29.

22. National Education Association, *The NEA Legislative Program for the 99th Congress* (Washington, D.C., July 1985), p. 5.

23. Ibid.

24. West, *The Power Base for Education*, pp. 179–80.

25. Interview with Dale Lestina.

26. Telephone interview with Michael Hill, Legislative Director for Congressman Dave Kildee (D-Mich.), Washington, D.C., September 3, 1986.

27. Ibid.

28. Ibid.

29. Telephone interview with Amy Shulz, Legislative Aide to U.S. Senator Quentin Burdick (D-N.D.), Washington, D.C., September 8, 1986.

30. Telephone interview with Deanna Marlowe, Legislative Aide to Senator Mark Andrews (R-N.D.), Washington, D.C., September 12, 1986.

31. Telephone interview with Sharon Matts, Administrative Assistant to Congressman Jack Brooks (D-Texas), Washington, D.C., September 12, 1986.

32. Telephone interview with John Conway, Congressional Contact Team Coordinator, National Education Association, Washington, D.C., February 13, 1987.

33. Ibid.

34. Ibid.

35. Interview with Rolland Dorfer, Regional Lobbyist, National Education Association, Norfolk, Va., October 14, 1985.

36. West, *The Power Base for Education*, p. 184.

37. Telephone interview with Dale Lestina, Political Specialist, National Education Association, Washington, D.C., September 22, 1986.

38. McLauglin and Catterall, "Notes on the New Politics of Education," p. 377.

39. Ibid.

40. Interview with Dr. Yvonne Miller, Assemblywoman, Virginia State Assembly, Norfolk, Va., November 25, 1985.

41. Interview with Dale Lestina.

42. Interview with Deanna Marlowe.

43. Interview with Dale Lestina.

44. Richard F. Elmore and Milbrey Wallin McLaughlin, *Reform and Retrenchment: The Politics of California School Finance Reform* (Cambridge, Mass.: Ballinger, 1982), p. 143.

45. Ibid.

46. Ibid., p. 144.

47. Ibid., pp. 92, 164.

48. Ibid., p. 92.

49. Ibid., pp. 100–101.

50. Ibid., p. 103.

51. Ibid.

52. Ibid., p. 117.

53. Ibid.

54. Ibid., p. 146.

55. Ibid., p. 164.

56. Shotts, "The Origin and Development of the National Education Association Political Action Committee, 1969–1976," p. 27.

57. Ibid., p. 38.

58. McGuire, "Politics 1980," p. 27.

59. *Today's Education*, February–March 1980, pp. 33–44.

60. Shotts, "The Origin and Development of the National Education Association Political Action Committee, 1969–1976," p. 83.

61. National Education Association, *You and Politics*, p. 12.

62. Ibid., p. 5.

63. Ibid.

64. National Education Association, *How To Set Up and Operate a Local Association Political Action Program* (Washington, D.C. 1985), p. 1.

65. National Education Association, *You and Politics*, p. 6.

66. Ibid., p. 7.

67. Ibid., p. 1.

68. Ibid., p. 6.

69. National Education Association, *How To Raise Money for NEA-PAC: Education's Defense Fund* (Washington, D.C., March 1985), p. 2.

70. Ibid., p. 1.

71. National Education Association, *How To Endorse Candidates* (Washington, D.C., September 1986), p. 3.

72. Ibid., p. 7.

73. National Education Association, *How To Recruit, Organize, and Manage Volunteers* (Washington, D.C., 1982), p. 1.

74. A. H. Raskin, "Teachers Now Lions in Political Arena," *New York Times*, January 15, 1975, p. 58.

75. National Education Association, *How To Run Voter Contact Programs* (Washington, D.C., 1982), p. 36.

76. National Education Association, *How To Conduct Opinion Polls* (Washington, D.C., 1982), p. 2.

77. National Education Association, *How To Participate in Party Politics* (Washington, D.C., 1981), p. 6.

78. Samuel L. Blumenfeld, *NEA: Trojan Horse in American Education* (Boise, Idaho: Paridigm, 1984) p. 207.

79. Chester E. Finn, Jr., "Teacher Politics," *Commentary*, February 1983, p. 39.

80. Interview with Joseph Standa, NEA Political Affairs Specialist, Washington, D.C., June 3, 1985.

81. Ibid.

82. Ibid.

83. Ibid.

84. Alec Gallup, "The Gallup Poll of Teacher Attitudes Toward the Public Schools," *Phi Delta Kappan*, October 1984, p. 101.

85. Interview with Joseph Standa.

86. Telephone interview with Ray Skuse, Director of Political Affairs, New York State United Teachers, AFL-CIO, Albany, N.Y., June 21, 1985.

87. Interview with Joseph Standa.

88. Letter from Rachelle Horowitz, Director AFT/COPE, to Donna Horton, National Commission on Election Information, October 17, 1984.

89. Tom Wicker, "20 Down Hill Years," *New York Times*, June 18, 1985, p. A27.

90. Interview with Joseph Standa.

91. Rachelle Horowitz, Director AFT/COPE, "Memorandum to AFT Executive Council and COPE Liaisons," March 11, 1985.

92. Ibid.

93. Lane Kirkland, AFL-CIO President, Memorandum to Affiliated Local Central Bodies, Washington, D.C., November 27, 1984, p. 1.

94. Ibid., p. 3.

95. Ibid., p. 1.

96. Horowitz, "Memorandum to AFT Executive Council and COPE Liaisons."

97. Blumenfeld, *NEA: Trojan Horse in American Education*, p. 173.

# 3

# The AFT: Number Two

The American Federation of Teachers, AFL-CIO, has also realized the importance of political power. The AFT attempts to implement its education agenda through its lobbying and through its political endorsements. However, the AFT is limited in its political impact by its size and resources. Most important, it is questionable how the AFT, as part of the AFL-CIO, can act independently as an agent for change in education.

What has been the success of the AFT politically? At best, one can conclude that the influence of the AFT in its support of political candidates is still growing. The union has aided in electing one president, Jimmy Carter in 1976, has increased its national effectiveness in recent years and is a power to be reckoned with in New York State. In the 1986 congressional and gubernatorial elections, the AFT achieved its best winning percentage in recent years: 80 percent of Senatorial and House candidates supported by the AFT won election.[1] The AFT locals in cities such as New York and Boston have helped elect mayors as well as governors in those states. In New York State, all backed candidates won in the state senate, and all but two won in the assembly, with all statewide office candidates winning.[2] We shall examine the New York State case more closely in the next chapter.

The first limitation of the AFT is size. The AFT numbers 600,000 members—one-third that of the NEA membership. The AFT strength is in the large cities of America. The AFT controls only one state, New York State, in teacher representation. Nevertheless, it is the collective bargaining representative in such megacities as New York, Boston, Philadelphia, Chicago, Washington, D.C., Detroit, San Francisco and St. Louis. The AFT was perceived as a strong teacher representative by teachers in the cities at a time when demographics indicated the exodus of a white middle class to the suburbs and their replacement by poor minorities. The militancy of the AFT, with its right to strike, appealed to teachers whose working conditions worsened as the poverty index rose.

The second limitation on the AFT is one of resources. Although contributions to the 1986 Committee on Political Education (COPE) had doubled in two years to $1 million—a sizeable sum—it was still half of the monies raised by the NEA.[3] The legislative staff of the AFT national headquarters is three full-time lobbyists, half that of the NEA.[4] And AFT's political action national staff is two full-time members, compared to six NEA representatives.

Still, the AFT has shown sporadic signs of political strength. In the 1980 presidential election, for example, more than fifty AFT members were elected delegates to the Democratic convention.[5] That same year, the New York State United Teachers were instrumental in the surprise upset victory in the Democratic primary for their candidate Senator Edward (Ted) Kennedy (D-Mass.). Thousands of teachers had served as Kennedy volunteers. Indeed, Kennedy thanked NYSUT, claiming that "without your support, I could not have won."[6] The political influence of the AFT is located mostly on the local and state levels; however, the AFT's presence as a national political force is becoming increasingly stronger, as the rise in COPE contributions attests.

Still the AFT was quick to learn its political lesson. After the breakthrough in collective bargaining in New York in 1961, the AFT considered supporting a mayoral candidate in 1965, and two full-time legislative representatives were hired to lobby in the state capitol. In his authorized study of the United Federation of Teachers (the New York City AFT affiliate) in 1974, the labor historian Philip Taft concluded that "political action has a high priority."[7] Professor Taft observed, "The UFT endorses candidates of state, national, and local offices, and the concern of its members about these matters may be measured by their contributions of almost $250,000 to 1972 campaigns."[8]

But the UFT and the AFT had a close role model for their political activity. Indeed, the labor movement had "invented" political activity, and its modern representative, the political action committee. In the 1936 presidential election, the Congress of Industrial Organizations mounted a controversial spending effort to back President Franklin D. Roosevelt. By 1943, the CIO had formalized its political thrust with the CIO-PAC—the first PAC in American history.[9] The merged AFL-CIO in the 1950s had its Committee on Political Education, and the AFT would create its national COPE in 1972.[10]

There were, moreover, informal signs of the growing political influence and awareness of the AFT. Professor Myron Lieberman in 1972 would observe the contact that New York's UFT would have with the world of politics. At the annual UFT luncheon, where some 3,000 teachers gathered, the dais was top-heavy with political "friends" of education. Lieberman counted five members of the U.S. House of Representatives, nine state senators, twenty-one members of the state assembly, the state attorney general and state comptroller, the deputy mayor and the city comptroller (who was subsequently to become mayor), and eight members of the city council.[11] This gathering caused Lieberman to wonder why the NEA "had avoided political leadership for so long."[12]

Lieberman drew a lesson from the UFT's acumen. "The level of public support for education," he commented, "is what politics is all about."[13] "Teachers can be slow learners, but they are finally getting the message: Treat education as 'nonpartisan' service and you cripple your efforts to fund it properly or to redirect it to more progressive objectives."[14]

But that lesson is still being learned. AFT affiliates vary in their degree of political sophistication. In Boston, for example, political effectiveness came late as compared to New York City. According to AFT Director of Field Services, Kim Moran, the Boston Teacher's Union only recently developed a "sustained, highly organized structure."[15] The Boston leadership became aware of the need to become involved in local and state elections. For example they successfully backed the Democratic challenger, Michael Dukakis, in the gubernatorial election.

## HISTORICALLY NUMBER TWO

Except for one brief moment when the AFT obtained collective bargaining in New York City, the AFT has been second to the NEA in leadership. From the beginning, the AFT perceived itself as part of the NEA. When the AFT was formed in 1916, the intent was to *reform* the NEA. Leaders of teacher groups from Chicago; New York; Gary, Indiana; Scranton, Pennsylvania; Washington, D.C.; and Oklahoma joined forces to create an organization made up wholly of teachers. In contrast, the NEA admitted supervisory personnel who, in turn, dominated the organization. AFT historian William E. Eaton concludes:

> Initially the American Federation of Teachers saw itself as more of a radical segment of the National Education Association than as a completely independent body. . . . Members were encouraged to attend the annual convention of the NEA.
> (One observer of) the day wrote: "There is considerable indication that these groups, at the outset, would have welcomed affiliation with the National Education Association either as departments or as adjunct organizations, but the reaction of the Association's management was one of horrified dismay."[16]

Still, the rationale of an organization that was strictly teachers was sound. To cement a worker's relationship, the AFT immediately applied for a charter from the American Federation of Labor, and President Samuel Gompers granted one. Forty-six years later, the obtaining of collective bargaining would propel the NEA into also becoming wholly a teacher organization.

Also from the start, the AFT would have a social hue. Founding members included the educator and philosopher John Dewey, and the educational and social reformer George Counts. In 1917, the *American Teacher* would look upon the "experiment" in Russia with utopian hopes for "democratic gains" of the Russian peasants and workers. "Russia: We Salute you in the name of the New Day" was the tribute on the front page of the *American Teacher*.[17]

This radical tinge caused problems in the early 1940s. Both the New York City Teachers Union and the Philadelphia AFT affiliate were expelled for alleged Communist domination. AFT rivals were

chartered, and in New York the Teacher's Guild was formed. Traces
of past radicalism linger. David Selden, former AFT President, has
long been active as a member of socialist groups, and AFT president Albert Shanker had been a member of the Socialist party in
his college days. Some current AFT staffers, such as COPE Director Rachelle Horowitz and UFT President Sandra Feldman, had
also been members of the Socialist party.[18] Still, for all its long
radical history, the AFT remains a centrist organization politically.
That is partly also the legacy of the Socialist movement in America,
which has moved from radical option to mainstream advocate.

The one notable exception when the AFT assumed educational
leadership was the breakthrough in collective bargaining in 1961.
It was the AFT New York City affiliate, the Teacher's Guild, that
would point the way for teacher unionism. Teacher unrest in New
York City schools and other urban school systems had been growing for a decade. Wages were low and teaching conditions were
worsening as demographic changes took place. Encouraged by federal policies in creating highways and offering low mortgage rates,
the predominatly white middle class exited to the suburbs, leaving
in their wake migrating poor minorities. Confronted with students
ravaged by poverty, teachers despaired over difficult teaching conditions.

Still, the initial spark did not come from a teacher union. Rather
an unaffiliated high school teacher's association finally called a strike
in New York City protesting wages and working conditions. Teacher
Guild leadership endorsed the night high school teachers' walkout,
despite fears of supporting a competitor. At this point the guild
leadership, under the direction of David Selden, forged the direction. Selden was the only paid, full-time staff member of the guild;
his position was under-written from funds from the AFL-CIO Industrial Union Department, which was under the control of Walter
Reuther, president of the United Auto Workers, who believed in
organizing teachers. Selden struck on a strategy of joining forces
into a merged union. The result was the new United Federation
of Teachers, AFL-CIO, which would harness the drive of the high
school teachers. Moreover, the radical taint the guild had carried
since the expulsion of Communist locals was washed away with the
creation of a new group.

The UFT changed its goal to collective bargaining rights. George

Meany, president of the AFL-CIO, however, was ambivalent about organizing teachers. Selden recalled that Meany had "a low opinion of teacher unions in general and the New York teachers organizations in particular."[19] Appeals to Meany for money went unheeded. Nevertheless, a successful strike for collective bargaining was held, and on December 2, 1961, the UFT won the subsequent collective bargaining election. The teacher rebellion had begun. Successive cities and suburbs were organized under the banner of the AFT or NEA within the next two decades.

After initially misreading the New York City breakthrough, the NEA followed suit, and most important, changed its structure to include teachers only. Still, for the most part, the AFT remains second to the NEA. Perhaps that is because the NEA was first a professional organization appealing to teacher psychology, whereas the AFT was a union stressing blue-collar issues. Now ironically, it is the AFT that makes more professional sounds and the NEA that has increased its emphasis on union concerns.

## LEGISLATION

The AFT, like the NEA, has had a long tradition of lobbying for desired educational legislation both on a national and local level. And the policy process on a national level for determining legislative goals is similarly democratic in nature to that of the NEA.

Legislation policy is established by AFT delegates at the bi-annual convention (until 1986, AFT conventions were held every year as in the NEA). Delegates from local and state affiliates submit their priorities to specific committees in charge of legislative matters. Delegates who wish to serve on these committees may do so. In turn, the committees refer legislative goals back to the convention delegates, who make the final determination.

Between conventions, the AFT Executive Council makes policy as the need arises, always working within the matrix of established convention policy. The AFT Executive Council is comprised of the AFT president and secretary-treasurer and thirty-four vice-presidents representing local and state affiliates. Day to day operation relating to legislative policy is the responsibility of the president and secretary-treasurer, who delegate the charge to the three full-time staff lobbyists.[20]

Current legislative policy seeks to preserve educational funding and withstand such educational thrusts as vouchers. The AFT has also taken positions on social and foreign policy matters. But the AFT has minced no words in criticizing the Reagan administration. In its 1984 compilation of the voting record of the 98th Congress, the AFT emphasized the legislative leadership of the president. The voting record of the 98th Congress (1982–1984), the AFT mused, "chronicles the second and hopefully, last two years of the Reagan Administration."[21] Whereas, the NEA in its criticism refrained from naming the president, the AFT was more bold:

The President's attempt to slash education spending by 50 percent failed in the 97th Congress. . . . But there is no doubt about Reagan's long-range goal, which is getting the Federal Government out of aiding public schools and into aiding private schools. . . . We can celebrate a major victory on the tuition tax credit bill, but it is plain that as long as Ronald Reagan occupies the White House, tuition tax credits will remain a dangerous possibility. . . . Only the election of Walter Mondale and strong Democratic House and Senate can put us back on the road to progress.[22]

The 98th Congress was divided in its political affiliation: the Senate was controlled by Republicans, the House, by Democrats. Nonetheless, in assessing the 98th Congress, the AFT concluded that the voting record of Congress "reflects the defensive posture that teachers and their unions have been forced to assume," an assessment the NEA concurred with.[23] The Reagan offensive on tuition tax credits, school prayer and cuts in educational funding offset the power of the teacher unions.

In its assessment of the 98th Congress, the AFT listed twelve priority legislative issues for both House and Senate. Since both houses differ in the specific bills introduced, the items may also differ. In the House, the AFT goals included maintaining education funding, opposing school prayer and slashing of social security benefits, enacting an equal rights amendment, opposing access by religious groups to public schools, providing domestic content legislation to protect American jobs, enacting fair tax reform, obtaining affordable telephone service, enacting a Civil Rights Act of 1984 and funding the National Endowment for Democracy.[24]

In the Senate, the AFT sought maintenance of education funding, opposing cuts in medicare, blocking transfer of teachers working for the Department of Defense and establishing a federal holiday honoring Dr. Martin Luther King, Jr. Other bills were similar to the House versions. The AFT rated the votes "right" or "wrong," depending on the AFT position, and absent votes were also recorded.[25]

In the 99th Congress (1984–1986), the AFT pursued ten legislative goals in the House and eight in the Senate. In the House, the AFT agenda included opposition to the Gramm-Rudman bill, which would require balancing the budget, enacting tax reform, establishing political rights for union members and obtaining pay equity for women. In the Senate, the AFT again opposed Gramm-Rudman-Hollings, a line item veto, and supported sanctions for South Africa and its policy of apartheid, and supported deducting state and local taxes in tax reform.[26] The AFT summed up its efforts in the 99th Congress by declaring that "the battle to lock Reaganism into the structure of the Federal government will become more intense as time runs out on the Reagan presidency."[27]

One issue in the 98th Congress that divided liberals and indicates the shift of the AFT to right of center was the funding of the National Endowment for Democracy (NED). Established in 1983, the NED functioned as a staunch anti-Communist agency in international affairs. It had been criticized as an agent of the Central Intelligence Agency, which sponsored some questionable right extremist groups in Europe.[28] The NED was bitterly opposed by some key Congressional liberals. Representative Richard Ottinger (D-N.Y.) was able to muster the necessary House support in 1984 to stop funding NED. In the Senate, however, Lowell Weicker (R-Conn.) failed to replicate the Ottinger victory.[29]

How successful has the AFT been in pursuing its educational and social agenda in Congress? In both the recent 98th and 99th Congresses, the results have been mixed. Of the twelve legislative priorities of the AFT in the 98th House of Representatives, the AFT saw its position win out in eight bills and lose in four; however, the four losses were major. They included cuts in social security funding that the AFT opposed, as well as having religious groups gain access to public schools. In addition, the AFT's support for an equal rights amendment did not pass the House.

In the Senate session, the AFT once more witnessed its position prevailing in eight issues and losing in four. The most significant losses involved the reduction of funds for medicare.

The AFT fared better in the 99th Congress, which again was dominated by Republicans in the Senate and by Democrats in the House. Of ten AFT priorities, only one was lost in the House. The AFT unsuccessfully opposed the Gramm-Rudman bill. In the Senate, the AFT was equally successful, losing again on the Gramm-Rudman-Hollings spending limits bill.

Some of the congressional victories in both houses were major. In the Senate, the AFT's opposition of a line item veto by the president on budget items was significant. In the House, the AFT opposition to reductions in student aid for college was also an important issue. And in both houses, the request for sanctions on South Africa as a means of condemning its policy of apartheid had wide repercussion. It must be pointed out that the AFT did not accomplish these congressional successes alone. In concert with the education lobby, and also with the wealthy and organized AFL-CIO, the AFT contributed to achieving its objectives.

The AFT has also been extremely influential legislatively in New York State. Let us examine how the AFT fared on its twelve item list in both houses of the 98th Congress in terms of the New York State delegation, where the AFT maintains strength. Of the thirty-four New York members of the House, all twenty-three Democrats and three of the eleven Republicans voted on the AFT side on most issues.[30] Senator Daniel Moynihan (D-N.Y.) voted "right" on 10 of 12 AFT priorities whereas his Republican colleague, Senator Alfonse D'Amato, split on the AFT agenda.[31] It must be pointed out, however, that New York is considered a politically "liberal" state.

The AFT attempts to galvanize support for its legislative programs among members on both a national and state level. To accomplish this, the AFT publishes a *Guide for Legislative Action and Collective Bargaining Laws*, which was written in the early 1970s and appears somewhat dated. Most of the guide deals with the status of collective bargaining in various states. Nevertheless, a small portion of the guide suggests techniques for applying pressure to legislators.

These legislative strategies differ considerably from those advocated by the NEA. Whereas the NEA stresses personal contact by members with legislators, the AFT manual emphasizes letter writing campaigns. The essence of an AFT campaign is collecting petitions, mounting rallies and promoting letter writing to legislators.

But in one respect the AFT manual is superior to the many fine publications of the NEA. The AFT manual suggests procedures for dealing with the press. This relationship has been a positive aspect of the AFT since its New York collective bargaining victory: AFT officials, especially President Albert Shanker, maintain excellent relations with the press. Consequently, the AFT has overshadowed the NEA in that respect. The AFT manual recommends to AFT members in charge of legislative campaigns that they establish "respectful relations" with the press.[32] The AFT manual writers understand the press. They remind AFT activists that the main task of a reporter is "to get a story" and that "the reporter will appreciate information from time to time" so that "you will not establish rapport if you ignore the press except when you want an article."[33] Moreover, the guide gives safe advice on how to conduct a press conference: Rule One is that an AFT spokesperson should "make no statement that you do not wish to have published."[34]

But it is the letter writing that is the centerpiece of the AFT legislative campaign. The authors of the AFT manual conclude that "next to personal contact, letters are the most effective method of communication."[35] Tips are given for such a campaign. Letters must be signed with addresses given so as to have greater impact on the specific legislator representing that constituency. Most important writers are advised to keep a letter short "and confine it to one issue."[36]

As a follow-up, AFT activists must apprise the membership of the actions of legislators, and AFT publications should publish summaries of voting records and important testimony from the Congressional Record.

In the final analysis, the legislative efforts of the AFT have not been as impressive as that of the rival NEA. Lacking the membership and resources of its rival, the AFT has yet to reach maximum effect in Congress and most state legislatures. However, the AFT is part of the larger education lobby, and on many issues upon which there is consensus, contributes a powerful force. Most important, the AFT has a distinct advantage as being a part of the

larger AFL-CIO in its effort to influence Congress and state legislatures.

## POLITICAL ACTION

There is a significant difference in the policy process for endorsing candidates in the AFT compared to that in the NEA. The AFT
process is more decentralized. Rather than have the national political body determine endorsements with state input, as in the NEA,
the national AFT accepts the recommendations of the local and
state bodies. There is one exception to this rule: When the local
bodies remain neutral in a race, the national COPE may endorse
a candidate.[37] On the other hand, the national office, with local
input, may exercise greater flexibility in endorsing a candidate for
president of the United States. The final determination to support
a presidential candidate rests with the delegates of the AFT convention; however, the AFT Executive Council may support a candidate in a primary before the convention meets. In the past four
presidential elections, the AFT has supported the Democratic
nominee.[38]

The policy process on a state level incorporates significant input
from local members. For example, in the primary for elections in
New York State in 1986, over 200 representatives from locals met
in Albany to consider endorsements. The staff of New York State
teachers union distributed up-to-date lists of declared candidates
and fact sheets on educational and social issues. The delegates had
already met regionally to discuss potential support. The recommendations of the convention delegates were presented to the New
York State United Teachers' (NYSUT) Political Education Committee and then to the board of directors for approval. After the primary, the state board of directors reviewed the results and considered other endorsements in the event of some lost primary
elections.[39]

The AFT has published guidelines for political activists that are
at some variance from those of the NEA. For one thing, the AFT
guidelines (issued in 1981) are more partisan. A *Guide to Political
Action* issued to members by the AFT's COPE warns that "these
are crisis times."[40] Moreover, the guide intones, "an insensitive
administration and a Republican-dominated Senate are threatening

public education's vital health programs, Social Security and other key projects."[41] The AFT guide is but one publication, in contrast to the series of twelve manuals on political action issued by the NEA. And for the most part, the AFT guide lacks the sophistication of the NEA series. For example, such exotic campaign strategies for volunteers as opinion polling and targeting are not discussed.

Still, there are similarities. The AFT guide stresses volunteers, fundraising, and operating phone banks. Most important, the AFT guide offers suggestions on forming coalitions. Although this information is mentioned in the NEA series, it is more detailed in the AFT manual.

The AFT guide presents a clear call for political action in these "crisis times." The AFT congratulates itself on being "considered one of the most politically effective organizations in the AFL-CIO."[42] Such a leadership role is needed in light of the fact that the AFT's traditional allies, "the Democratic leadership in the House and Senate, [have] shown us how *not* to act in a crisis."[43] According to the AFT, Congress had "fallen prey to White House rhetoric that claims there was a mandate in November (1980)."[44]

Nevertheless, the AFT manual cautions against voting for a person simply because he or she may be liberal. "It is wrong to endorse a candidate because he or she is 'progressive,' " the manual intones, and "it is equally wrong to withhold an endorsement because the candidate is 'right wing.' "[45] What matters is the candidate's position and voting record, if such be the case, on education and related social issues. In the final analysis, the implication, nevertheless, is that the AFT favors centrist liberals.

The first task of the guide is for activists to form a Committee on Political Education (COPE). Sample resolutions and a constitution are presented. The COPE local committee is to consist of local officers plus individuals who are either volunteers or appointed by the local president and serve for two-year terms.

In order for a candidate to obtain a COPE endorsement, he or she must be selected "solely on the basis of each candidate's record on labor, health, education and various policy issues without regard to party affiliation."[46] The primary aim of labor in that declaration suggests that the AFT has a larger agenda as part of the AFL-CIO. In endorsements priority is given to supporting incumbents with a pro–AFT legislative program and to opposing incumbents who, in turn, are "overwhelmingly in opposition to the AFT's program."[47] In the event there are no incumbents, the local COPE may consider refraining from endorsing anyone—an option not suggested in the NEA materials. Endorsements require a two-thirds vote of the local executive board or delegate assembly.

Campaign fund raisers are urged in the guide to establish a system-wide check-off procedure for contributions where feasible. Under this arrangement, the school system automatically deducts COPE contributions and forwards them to the AFT local. The guide then lists eight steps in fund raising and discusses them at some length. These include: identify political issues that affect teachers, develop a theme from these concerns, establish a time line for contributions, start the campaign with letters to members, alert members through weekly literature, design an incentive program for activists to sign up members as volunteers, and finally to "pat yourself on the back" for completing a fund raising drive.[48]

Two other significant issues are addressed in the guide. First, the relationship of the AFT to the AFL-CIO is probed. The guide notes that "throughout this manual, working with the AFL-CIO has been stressed."[49] The lesson is clear. "Working together under the umbrella of the AFL-CIO," the guide proclaims, "political strength and effectiveness expands a hundredfold."[50] The other important issue is forming coalitions. Six practical steps to organizing a coalition in the community are outlined. The AFT guide places great emphasis on the need for the local COPE to exert, through coalitions, the broadest political impact.

The guide's section on volunteers is not as extensive as the separate NEA manual on the topic but is no less important. According to the AFT, "volunteers are the key to AFT political activity."[51] Eight steps are given for AFT activists to recruit managers and retain volunteers. These include insuring pleasant surroundings, planning, making reasonable assignments, providing sufficient training, offering opportunities for greater responsibility, praising volunteers, and scheduling an after elections party. In this latter respect, the AFT strategy departs once again from NEA guidelines. The AFT suggests that volunteers be congratulated for their efforts at every opportunity—a technique in human relations in which the NEA is silent.

In similar fashion, suggestions for operating a phone bank are commonsensical. Volunteers are urged to be polite and never argue. They are instructed never to call after 9 P.M., never to leave messages with children; moreover, they should keep messages short and maintain an accurate record of people telephoned. Most important, volunteers are reminded that "the telephone is the voice of the union and/or candidate."[52] Samples are provided on how to conduct a telephone survey.

An additional section in the guide is devoted to the legal aspects of political contributions. This topic is not discussed in the NEA materials. It is pointed out that local affiliates cannot spend monies from the regular account but may use general fund money for some services. These include communicating with members, registration campaigns and paying salaries to staff members assigned to the local COPE.

Finally, the guide poses stock questions and provides answers. A consistent question concerns affiliation with the AFL-CIO. The guide argues that labor affiliation "pools the resources of 120 international and national unions."[53] Equally important is the question of the AFT's drift to the Democratic party. The guide provides this exchange:

Q. I am a Republican. Why should I support my local's endorsed candidates when so many of the candidates are Democrats (or vice-versa)?

A. Local and AFT-COPE are nonpartisan and intend to remain nonpartisan. Political party affiliation is not a consideration in endorsements. Voting records on education, labor and health issues are the determinants for selection.[54]

The only other AFT publication of a political nature is a rather detailed and intelligent manual on voter registration; however, one wonders for whom the manual is intended. The broad implication is that is it meant to facilitate the voter registration of AFT members. But, as the manual points out in its review of the research on who registers and votes, college educated citizens are among the highest percentage of voters. In polls taken in 1983 and 1984, only one-sixth of college grads were not registered, the lowest percentage of any group.[55] Moreover, from 85 to 90 percent of teachers vote regularly.[56] This manual could best serve teacher activists seeking to expand voter registration among lower socioeconomic groups that traditionally have a poor record of voting.

Nonetheless, the registration manual, entitled *Register and Vote: The Future Depends on It*, provides a valuable service. Again, the guide is time bound having been prepared before the 1984 presidential election. The manual warns that "the issues at stake in the upcoming November elections are critical to union members."[57] A four-point registration campaign is planned. First, COPE activists are to familiarize themselves with registration law, which varies from state to state. Second, activists are to prepare membership lists and assign canvassers. Third, materials are prepared to advertise registration dates and sites. And fourth, the registration drive is to be publicized through union media.

Registration procedures differ in a number of states. Twenty-two states require only mail registration. Others are handled by deputy registrars. Still other states may handle registration at a central facility or may delegate the responsibility to a branch office. Some voters only register on election day. It is up to the AFT activist to know the proper procedures. For example, with deputy registrars, the AFT manual suggests that activists discover who can be deputized. In addition, the AFT activist should inquire whether an election board official can train and deputize union canvassers. The AFT guidelines in this section are quite knowledgeable.

The next step is planning. "Planning," the manual tells us, "means thinking it through."[58] Guidelines are suggested. These include meeting with the COPE committee to decide to have a voter registration drive. Then the COPE committee meets with local election officials to determine ground rules and assigns union stewards and building representatives as canvassers. In addition, a publicity campaign is established: posters are placed, articles on the drive are published in the union newspaper and follow-up telephone calls are made to union members to remind them to register. Finally, canvassers meet to report the results of the drive.

Canvassers obtain membership lists of AFT members at schools. These are then matched with official voter registration rolls. Common arguments voiced by teachers against registering are considered. Teachers may tell canavassers that they do not want to register for fear of having to serve on a jury. Or they may insist that their individual vote does not make a difference. Or they may charge that politics is corrupt by nature. According to the AFT guide, canvassers are to counter by pointing out that jury selection depends also on other citizen lists. And they can claim that "one vote does make a difference . . . (since) . . . voting changed the country after the Great Depression."[59] Moreover, according to the AFT guide, "voting is the way to keep politicians honest."[60]

There are other tips for canvassers. They should make personal contact with the AFT member to discern his or her registration status. In discussing the importance of registrating a canvasser should be positive and refrain from argumentation. The canvasser must avoid embarrassing the union member in the event that he or she is not registered. In addition, the canvasser is provided with a kit with useful information. This includes facts on registration law, forms, answers to frequently asked questions, a list of union members and message outlines.

An appendix in the manual provides helpful information. The 1980 registration results in each state are given. Date requirements in each state, and demographic polls on unregistered voters are discussed. Finally there is a memo from COPE "wherein it is demonstrated with convincing evidence that those who gripe that one-vote-doesn't-count-so-why-bother are greviously in error."[61]

## RELATIONSHIP TO THE AFL-CIO

Perhaps the most controversial aspect of the AFT has been its relationship to the AFL-CIO. As part of the larger labor movement, there is some question whether the AFT can function independently. The evidence suggests that although there are some benefits to be accrued from the relationship to the AFL-CIO, there have been instances where the AFT has not fully functioned independently of the AFL-CIO, when conflict between the two groups arises.

Critics, especially those within the NEA, claim that the AFL-CIO affiliation undermines the professionalism of teacher groups. The irony has been that the NEA has slightly moved from its emphasis on "professionalism" toward unionism, whereas the AFT is now making stronger movement toward professionalism. Still, one critic, the journalist Robert Braun, believes that the AFT is not competent, as a result of being a union, to lead in education. He writes:

The union hardly has displayed a depth of understanding of either the political or educational process which would motivate a community willingly to turn over its schools to its kindly command. And there is little in its history, its present operations or its leadership to indicate that the AFT would know what to do with the public schools of the nation should it manage to assume control.[62]

The argument advanced by Braun was that the AFT, as an AFL-CIO union, was little interested in education and more concerned with satisfying more mundane blue collar aims. (Parenthetically, Braun's book, *Teachers and Power*, published in 1972, nowhere discusses the emerging political power of either the AFT nor the NEA.)

What bothers concerned observers of the AFL-CIO is the pursuing of narrow self-interests by the labor federation. According to its critics, it is this tunnel vision that has caused the labor movement to decline sharply in the past generation. From 25 percent of the work force in the 1950s, the labor movement has declined to 18 percent of the work force by 1985.[63] Moreover, the decline has been sharpest among the young—the hope of the future for labor. In 1985 only 16.7 percent of the young joined unions, compared to 18.2 percent in 1984.[64]

The reasons for the decline are compounded. First, the pursuit of narrow blue-collar policies by the AFL-CIO at a time when the work force was turning white collar was bad policy. In 1956, the United States ceased to be a manufacturing economy and became a service-oriented, postindustrial system. Labor was slow to respond. Under the leadership of George Meany, a New York plumber, the AFL-CIO resisted white collar and professional organizing. This resistance was especially true of teachers.

Meanwhile the 1960s brought on an ideological crisis. The AFL-CIO, under Meany's helm, found itself out of favor with the young activists of the sixties. The AFL-CIO's support of the Vietnam War and promoting a hard line anti-Communism, plus opposing affirmative action and being slow to champion the civil rights movement, alienated a generation whom many observers considered the most socially conscious since the Great Depression. The historian of the AFT characterized the conservative policies of the AFL-CIO during that time as "stodgy."[65]

By the late seventies and early eighties, other problems beset the labor movement. The bedrock of the AFL-CIO, those blue-collar industries of steel and auto, were in decline as a consequence of fierce competition from abroad. Structural changes were taking place in the economy. The "smokestack" industries with high union wages and benefits were in serious erosion. The new economy highlighted "high tech" industries, where workers were paid less and least likely to unionize. The AFL-CIO was behind the times.

Moreover, the labor movement became victim to the conservative political revolution that attended the Reagan Presidency. A sign of the times was President Reagan's firing of the air traffic controllers during their strike that crippled a union that was one of the few which had supported him. And with deregulation, industries such as the airline industry reorganized through bankruptcy proceedings to avoid the high cost of unionization in order to compete with new low cost carriers. In addition, industries moved from the unionized South and Southwest. The labor movement was truly in crisis.

Through it all, the AFL-CIO had not altered its blue collar agenda. One radical sociologist, Stanley Aronowitz, charged the AFL-CIO leadership as having done the following:

pursued narrow self-interest, and bought into the corparatist system, instead of building a strong labor movement to oppose it. The labor movement is not a labor movement at all, but a collection of insurance companies parading as unions.[66]

Most important, the AFL-CIO endured a schism within its ranks. Walter Reuther, President of the United Automobile Workers and former head of the CIO, bolted his union from the AFL-CIO. Reuther, a rival to Meany, expressed "his dissatisfaction with what has happened to labor movement" since merger in 1955.[67]

Reuther represented a more socially conscious and daring segment of labor. Reuther had encouraged the growth of teacher unionism from his Industrial Union Department, which funneled funds to key teacher locals to pay staff salaries for organizers. This funding was being done at a time when George Meany was dubious of teacher or white-collar organization. Understandably, former AFT President David Selden "agreed with all of Reuther's charges" but felt that "the AFT could not afford to alienate itself from the mainstream of the labor movement."[68]

On the other hand, supporters of the AFL-CIO, including the current AFT leadership, still perceive the labor movement as constituting the single largest *institution* in America seeking to promote the social good. Nevertheless, these supporters refrain from advocating deep change in the direction of the AFL-CIO. AFT officials consider the relationship to the AFL-CIO to be imperative.

The NEA has criticized this relationship from both ends of the political spectrum at different times in its history. Prior to the rise of teacher unionism, in the sixties, the NEA perceived the AFL-CIO as being too far to the left. After its transformation into a teacher's union, the NEA shifted gears and considered the organized labor movement as being to the political right of NEA policies.

The AFT has a history of hewing closely to the AFL-CIO political line. There have been two notable exceptions. One major exception occurred in 1972 when the AFT, under Selden's leadership, endorsed Senator George McGovern (D-S.D.) for the presidency. McGovern had made the ending of the Vietnam War his major goal. On the other hand, George Meany and the AFL-CIO leadership fully supported the war. Although McGovern had the better record on labor issues, the AFL-CIO favored Senator Henry Jackson (D-Wash.). Jackson was the type of hard-line anti-Communist the leadership of the AFL-CIO preferred. When McGovern became the choice of the Democratic Convention, the AFL-CIO took the unprecedented step of remaining neutral in the race.

The AFT took another course. Under Selden's direction, the delegates to the 1972 AFT Convention overwhelmingly endorsed the candidacy of McGovern. This was the first presidential endorsement by any teacher union. And it was achieved despite the opposition of Albert Shanker, president of the New York local, who sided with the AFL-CIO and opposed McGovern.

Selden was to pay a price for his independence. Although McGovern would also receive the support of 33 other unions, Meany did not take Selden's defection lightly. Consequently, he bypassed Selden and appointed Albert Shanker, the head of a *local* union, to an AFL-CIO Vice Presidency on the Executive Council. The ploy strengthened Shanker's ambitions to become AFT president. Shanker already enjoyed a certain measure of notoriety for his opposition to black community control in New York City, and his image among teachers began to eclipse that of Selden. Most important, the ascendancy of Shanker to the AFT presidency would bring the AFT more into line with the conservative policies of the AFL-CIO. Selden was clear on where he stood:

The AFT could best serve the interests of teachers, American society and the labor movement by not allowing itself to be co-opted by the conservative AFL-CIO leadership. . . . Therefore, the AFT should align itself with the liberals in the labor movement and in society in general.[69]

The result was that in 1974 Albert Shanker defeated Selden for the AFT presidency and has retained that office to this day.

One minor departure of the AFT from the leadership of the AFL-CIO occurred in the 1980 presidential race. Shanker and the AFT leadership decided to support the candidacy of Senator Edward Kennedy in the Democratic primary. The ultra-liberal Kennedy seemed an odd choice for the AFT, until one considered that the NEA was once again endorsing the incumbent President Jimmy Carter. Many observers felt that the AFT position was a gamble to exert influence not to be shared by its rival. On the other hand, the AFL-CIO refrained from endorsing a primary candidate, although one may assume that Kennedy would not have been their first choice. The AFL-CIO ended that policy in 1984 and endorsed a presidential primary candidate, former Vice President Walter Mondale.

Nevertheless, for the most part, the AFT and the AFL-CIO maintain similar policies and politics. One AFL-CIO staffer points out, for example, that on legislative matters the two organizations are "usually synchronized."[70] It is unlikely with the present leadership that the AFT will significantly adopt a more independent course.

## NOTES

1. Telephone interview with Rachelle Horowitz, Director of the Committee on Political Education (COPE), American Federation of Teachers, AFL-CIO, Washington, D.C., December 3, 1986.

2. *New York Teacher*, September 29, 1986, pp. 6–7; *New York Times*, November 6, 1986, pp. 14–15.

3. Interview with Rachelle Horowitz.

4. Telephone interview with Gerald Morris, Associate Director of Legislation, American Federation of Teachers, AFL-CIO, December 1, 1986.

5. "Challenge of the 1980s: A Political Report," *American Teacher*, September 1980, p. 6.

6. Ibid., p. 4.

7. Philip Taft, *United They Teach: The Story of the United Federation of Teachers* (Los Angeles: Nash Publishing, 1974), p. 231.

8. Ibid.

9. Larry J. Sabato, *PAC Power: Inside the World of Political Action Committees* (New York: W. W. Norton, 1984), p. 7.

10. Telephone interview with Robert Porter, Secretary-Treasurer, American Federation of Teachers, AFL-CIO, Washington, D.C., February 10, 1987.

11. Myron Lieberman, "The Union Merger Movement: Will 3,500,000 Teachers Put It All Together?" *Saturday Review*, June 24, 1972, p. 52.

12. Ibid., p. 53.

13. Ibid.

14. Ibid., p. 52.

15. "Political Action: The Miracle Worker," *American Teacher*, October 1986, p. 4.

16. William Edward Eaton, *The American Federation of Teachers, 1916–1961* (Carbondale: Southern Illinois University Press, 1975), p. 18.

17. *American Teacher*, April 1917, p. 1.

18. Maurice R. Berube, "Democratic Socialists and the Schools," *New Politics*, Summer 1969.

19. David Selden, *The Teacher Rebellion* (Washington, D.C.: Howard University Press, 1985), p. 46.

20. Interview with Gerald Morris.

21. American Federation of Teachers, AFL-CIO, *Voting Record 1984: The AFT Rates the 98th Congress* (Washington, D.C., 1985), p. 1.

22. Ibid.

23. Ibid.

24. Ibid., pp. 2–3.

25. Ibid.

26. American Federation of Teachers, AFL-CIO, *Voting Record 1986: The AFT Rates the 99th Congress* (Washington, D.C., 1986), p. 1.

27. Ibid.

28. *New York Times*, June 1, 1986, p. 1.

29. American Federation of Teachers, *The AFT Rates the 98th Congress*, pp. 3–4.

30. Ibid., pp. 2–3.

31. Ibid., p. 4.

32. American Federation of Teachers, AFL-CIO, *Guide for Legislative Action and State Collective Bargaining Laws* (Washington, D.C., 1975), p. 15.

33. Ibid.

34. Ibid.

35. Ibid., p. 17.

36. Ibid.

37. Interview with Rachelle Horowitz.

38. Telephone interview with Gregory Humphrey, Director of Legislation, American Federation of Teachers, AFL-CIO, Washington, D.C., December 3, 1986.

39. *New York Teacher*, September 1, 1986, p. 6.

40. American Federation of Teachers, *A Guide to Political Action* (Washington, D.C., September 1981), p. 5.

41. Ibid.

42. Ibid., p. 6.

43. Ibid., p. 5.

44. Ibid., pp. 6–7.

45. Ibid.

46. Ibid., p. 10.

47. Ibid.

48. Ibid., p. 17.

49. Ibid., p. 19.

50. Ibid.

51. Ibid., p. 22.

52. Ibid., p. 23.

53. Ibid., p. 30.

54. Ibid.

55. American Federation of Teachers, *Register and Vote: The Future Depends on It* (Washington, D.C., 1984), p. 37.

56. Jerome Cramer, "Here's How Teacher Power Affects You," *American School Board Journal*, November 1980, p. 35.

57. Ibid., p. 4.

58. Ibid., p. 8.

59. Ibid., pp. 13–14.

60. Ibid.

61. Ibid., p. 30.

62. Robert J. Braun, *Teachers and Power: The Story of the American Federation of Teachers* (New York: Simon and Schuster, 1972), pp. 244–45.

63. *New York Times*, February 8, 1986, p. 28.

64. Ibid.

65. Eaton, *The American Federation of Teachers, 1916–1961*, p. 194.

66. Karen J. Winkley, "Precipitous Decline of American Unions Fuels Growing Interest Among Scholars," *Chronicle of Higher Education*, November 12, 1986, p. 16.

67. Selden, *The Teacher Rebellion*, p. 164.

68. Ibid.

69. Ibid.

70. Telephone interview with Beulah Carter, Staff Assistant, Research Department, AFL-CIO, Washington, D.C., November 14, 1986.

# 4

# Teacher Power:
# Case Studies

Perhaps the best way to examine the dialectic of teacher politics is to consider case studies. We shall review case studies on the local, state and national levels. We shall look at presidential politics and, finally, the limits of political teacher power. In all cases, except in local politics, we shall examine political contests. On a local level, it would behoove us to assess the impact of the teachers' unions on school politics—the election of members to local school boards. Although the teacher unions, and the AFT affiliates in particular, are increasingly involved in mayoral elections in such cities as New York and Boston, it would be more appropriate to examine local school politics.

## LOCAL SCHOOL POLITICS

Local school boards control much of educational policy in the United States. With powers over budget, curriculum and personnel, these boards shape educational policies. Moreover, local school boards are elected in every state of the union except in Virginia (which is now considering the option of election). Consequently, teacher unions are extremely concerned with who serves on these boards. Both the NEA and AFT endorse local school board candidates in hopes of exerting influence.

This power of school politics is no more apparent than in New York City. The New York AFT affiliate, the United Federation of

Teachers, has proven to be immensely influential in local school politics. This is all the more ironic since the UFT was the chief opponent of elected boards when the issue arose in the community control struggle in the late 1960s. But with the enactment of a decentralization law in New York State in 1969, thirty-two Community School Boards were to be elected in New York City.

The community control advocates, (of which I was one), had recommended to the state legislature that *only* parents with children in public schools be permitted to vote for members of the school boards. The underlying theory of the key study, written by Mayor John Lindsay's Advisory Committee on School Decentralization, sought to restrict voter eligibility and infuse the schools with new parental energy and interest. Moreover, the stratagem intended to empower a low-income population, mostly black and hispanic, that accounted for the large majority of students, to become part of the school's democratic process. The community control plan came under heavy fire, largely from the UFT. In the final analysis, the legislature compromised and established school elections that allowed all citizens to vote under a complicated proportional representation system. Proportional representation, however, in practice, favored highly organized groups.

The initial result was a disaster. The first community school board elections favored slate voting, where 80 percent of the slates won.[1] Consequently, the most organized groups captured the elections, sometimes with school districts that were mostly black having mostly white school board representation. The two most organized groups in the first elections proved to be, ironically, first the Catholic Church, and second, the UFT. The Catholic Church readily saw an opportunity to divert resources to its own school system. As a result, the slates sponsored by the Catholic Church won the most elections, followed by that of the UFT.

Of the 279 community school board members elected in 1970, 201 were white, 47 were black, 30 were Puerto Rican, and one was Chinese.[2] Of these, 50.6 percent were Catholic, 36 percent were Jewish, and 11.2 percent were Protestant.[3] The most common profile of the school board member was that of a white, male Catholic, professionally trained, with at least two children in parochial schools, and living in the district for about nine years.[4]

The UFT was second in influence. It was directly responsible for electing 46 of the 279 school board members.[5] More important, the UFT in this first school board election "could more easily defeat a candidate than put their [sic] slate over."[6] The UFT, according to a study by Marilyn Gittell, me and others, was "thus without question, a powerful force in all community school districts."[7] However, it was especially powerful in this first election in 19 of 31 school districts.[8] This, despite the fact that the pupil population in those districts was overwhelmingly poor, black and Hispanic, and that only three of the nineteen UFT influenced districts had white majorities.[9]

In the intervening years, the UFT consolidated its school political power. By 1986, the UFT had become the dominant force in New York City school politics. In the May 1986 Community School Board elections, UFT backed candidates won majorities in 25 of 32 school boards. UFT candidates won 183 of the 288 school board seats. This influence was even more noticeable in the boroughs of Brooklyn and Queens. UFT candidates won 75 of the 108 school board seats in Brooklyn; in Queens, UFT supported candidates won 47 of the 63 school board positions.[10]

Moreover, the UFT captured all nine seats in four community school districts. These were District 1, Manhattan, in the Lower East Side with a largely poor school population comprised mostly of Puerto Ricans, but with sizeable numbers of Chinese, black and Italian students; District 25 in Queens, a mostly white, middle-class community with an increasing number of middle-class Asians; District 14 in Brooklyn, a mostly poor Puerto Rican school population with a sizeable black minority; and District 21 in Brooklyn, a largely poor black school population with a sizeable Puerto Rican minority.[11]

In only two board elections was the UFT badly defeated. In District 7 of the Bronx, a largely poor Puerto Rican community, the UFT supported no candidates. It was the only community school board district of the thirty-two that the UFT did not field a slate of candidates. In District 5, Manhattan, the heart of Harlem, the most famous of America's black ghettos, only three UFT candidates won election on the nine-person board.[12]

By early 1987, a movement was underway to eliminate the Community School Board elections in New York City. Spearheaded by Robert Wagner, Jr., the president of the New York City Board of

Education (and son of a popular mayor of the 1950s and 1960s), Wagner declared that the board would request the state legislature to abolish the elections and decentralization. Wagner concluded that the city's decentralized system was susceptible to patronage by the local boards and that "low voter turnouts in school board elections . . . mean organized interest groups often control policy."[13] In addition, Wagner cited the high cost of elections as added reason to eliminate the process. On the other hand, Jose E. Serrano, chairman of the Education Committee of the State Assembly, announced that he would introduce legislation that would accomplish the opposite. Serrano proposed to eliminate the complicated system of proportional representation that favors organized interest groups. The UFT's reaction was to preserve a system that has served them well through the years. UFT President Sandra Feldman declared, "I don't think we should swing the pendulum all the way back to where it was before decentralization."[14]

## STATE POLITICS

The AFT controls but one state in teacher membership—New York, but it provides an admirable case study of effective teacher politics. The New York City local, the United Federation of Teachers, was an early political influence in city and state. In 1972, the New York local merged with the state NEA affiliate, to become the New York State United Teachers. In time, the AFT captured control of the merged union and the NEA withdrew. Now, NYSUT processes a sophisticated and enlarged political staff of over a half dozen professionals and has been a key actor in New York State politics.

Nowhere was that key role more evident than in the 1986 congressional and state elections. NYSUT was not only effective in its support of candidates, but put in an early bid in its influence with a possible presidential candidate, Governor Mario Cuomo. Governor Cuomo had become a household name as a result of his electrifying speech at the 1984 Democratic Convention. He had earned a reputation in public office as a moderate with wide support. The AFT's forceful support of Cuomo insured the union of an inside track in the future, should he become a Democratic nominee and, possibly, president of the United States.

Nevertheless, it is in state politics that NYSUT exerts considerable influence. New York State has been traditionally a liberal state
with large cities such as New York Ciy as a base. Still, there is a
sprinkling of upstate moderate and conservative Republicans.
Democrats traditionally dominate the national offices, whereas in
the legislature, Republicans have dominated the senate. On the
other hand, the assembly, with its large New York City block, usually is Democratic. NYSUT pragmatically supports both Democrats
and Republicans.

In the 1986 elections, NYSUT's Board of Directors endorsed 17
congressional candidates, 56 state senate candidates, and a governor, lieutenant governor, attorney general, and comptroller.[15] Of
interest is the fact that they refrained from endorsing a candidate
for the U.S. Senate. The Democratic challenger to conservative
Republican Senator Alphonse D'Amato was Mark Green of New
York City. Green, once associated with consumer advocate Ralph
Nader, proved too liberal in his positions for NYSUT.

NYSUT scored a large success in the elections. Of the New York
City candidates in the Democratic primaries, nineteen of twenty-
one supported by the City United Federation of Teachers won—a
success rate greater than 90 percent.[16] In the state, 94 percent of
NYSUT-backed candidates in both Democratic and Republican
primaries won.[17] Most important, of the thirty-one contested elections, twenty-nine candidates endorsed by NYSUT won.[18] The ability
of the union to aid candidates in contested elections indicates its
powerful impact.

The state elections replicated the primaries. In the congressional
elections, NYSUT supported fourteen Democrats and one Republican.[19] Only two lost. One of those who lost challenged the conservative Republican incumbent, Congressman Jack Kemp, who
had become a national figure and a contender for the Republican
presidental nomination in 1988. NYSUT supported four challengers, and two won congressional seats.

In the Republican-controlled Senate in the state legislature, NY-
SUT endorsed 32 Republicans and 23 Democrats, all of whom won.[20]
In the New York Assembly, NYSUT supported 49 Republicans and
76 Democrats, only two of whom lost.[21] However, in both houses,
NYSUT only supported incumbents. This reinforces the thesis of
critics that PACs tend to favor incumbents. On the other hand, it

is a testimony to the stability of New York State politics. The endorsed candidates for state offices from governor to comptroller all won.

The state legislature candidates endorsed by NYSUT were chosen on the basis of their pro-union educational record in the legislature, "This [endorsement] is based on NYSUT program bills that the union supported vigorously," commented Ron Frantz, assistant to the NYSUT executive president. "On average, 35 or 40 votes provide the litmus test."[22]

Perhaps the most important NYSUT endorsement was for Governor Mario Cuomo's re-election campaign. Governor Cuomo was considered a major contender for the Democratic presidential nomination in 1988. Indeed, a poll in early 1987 had only two major Democratic choices: former Senator Gary Hart, whose campaign would soon be derailed, leading with 33 percent of the Democratic vote and Cuomo, a solid second, with 17 percent of the vote.[23] Other candidates did not figure significantly in the poll. NYSUT and the AFT had established significant influence with a possible future president of the United States.

NYSUT support of Cuomo came early and strong. By May of 1986, NYSUT was the fifth largest contributor to the governor's re-election campaign fund since his first election in January 1983. NYSUT had contributed $41,000.[24] By the election, NYSUT had become the second largest contributor—following an investment banker—with $104,845.[25] Unions were high on the list of Cuomo contributors, and NYSUT was both first and foremost. Such devotion could not be forgotten in both state and, perhaps, national politics.

NYSUT leaders considered Cuomo a friend to education. He was cited as having "championed programs to strengthen teaching and to improve public education."[26] Public schools had received more than $1.5 billion in increased state aid in the last three years. Moreover, Cuomo was credited by NYSUT as having "spearheaded the historic 'Excellence in Teaching' program," which added another $95 million to improve teachers salaries.[27]

Nevertheless, not all teacher unionists were enthusiastic. Nuala M. Drescher, president of the AFT's United University Professions, considered Cuomo's cuts in higher education in 1986, to "create real pain and suffering."[28] Drescher concluded that Cuomo's plan for colleges and universities "would have been a disaster."[29]

Cuomo's re-election was regarded as a "shoo-in."[30] He benefited by a politically weak Republican opponent, Andrew O'Rourke from Westchester County, who had little support from President Reagan; moreover, Cuomo had the superior resources. The governor had organized an $8 million campaign fund drive, whereas O'Rourke could only muster $1.2 million.[31] Cuomo's aides expected to retain about $4 million in the treasury for a possible presidential campaign.[32]

The campaign was tepid. Neither candidate drew sharp issues. Cuomo campaigned on a promised cut in personal taxes, building more prisons, increasing state aid to local school districts and renewing New York City's rent guidelines—an agenda that a Republican could find congenial. O'Rourke campaigned on combating drugs, making the state economically competitive, and creating jobs—a program that a Democrat could approve.[33]

What was important to the governor was the size of the re-election victory. A substantial victory could mean added momentum in a possible presidential race. Observers considered a "big victory" would add up to 60 percent for Cuomo and 40 percent for O'Rourke.[34] The governor exceeded those expectations. He received 65 percent of the 2.68 million votes cast, with a large 1.34 million plurality.[35] It was the widest margin of victory in the history of New York State.

Still, there were critics. Fellow Democratic candidates for state offices grumbled that the governor had not campaigned strongly enough to help their cause. Cuomo had adopted a "rose garden" strategy for his re-election. He avoided debates and minimized his campaigning on the theory that he didn't want to give his opponent media exposure. Although this strategy proved successful for him, it may have damaged the chances of other Democratic candidates who needed strong support from the governor. Democratic hopes were high that a Cuomo landslide might carry Democrats to gain control of the traditionally Republican state senate. In the end, Republicans retained control of the senate, and in the traditionally Democratic assembly, the Democrats increased their majority by only one seat—and in a narrow victory in Rochester at that.[36]

Moreover, the press reportage of the criticism provoked Cuomo. The governor has always been sensitive to press criticism.[37] After the election he accused the press of being biased against him. Such actions could be self-defeating for a person in need of a good press in search of the highest office in the land.

Ideologically, Cuomo is slightly to the left of the AFT leadership. Still, one must remember that the AFT enthusiastically supported Senator Edward Kennedy in the 1980 Democratic presidential primaries. Senator Kennedy had been much more liberal in his positions than Governor Cuomo. For the AFT leadership, it might just be a case of a pragmatic gamble—supporting a possible winner.

There is some evidence that Governor Cuomo had gained that broad appeal to be just such a winner. In a nation where only Lyndon Johnson, among Democratic presidents since Franklin Roosevelt, has won a majority of white votes, Cuomo appears to have appeal for that white majority. Two political scientists from Marist College, (a small Catholic college in Poughkeepsie, New York) have analyzed the 1986 gubernatorial data and concluded that such is the case. According to Lee M. Miringoff and Barbara Carvalho, Cuomo has strong support from New York suburban voters, an indication of his strength outside the traditional Democratic constituencies. Although Cuomo has taken himself out of the 1988 presidential race, he has left open the possibility of running in 1992.

## PRESIDENTIAL POLITICS

The key political event of teacher politics was the NEA's endorsement of Governor Jimmy Carter for President of the United States in 1976. That political event thrust teacher unions into the political limelight. Although the AFT had previously endorsed Senator George McGovern (D-S.D.) in 1972, scant attention was paid to the fact. Moreover, critics of the NEA's entry into presidential politics spared similar action of the AFT.

The reasons for strong opposition to the NEA's presidential politics were clear. As the largest union in America, the NEA was an intimidating opponent. Most important, the NEA's drift to the left angered a budding conservative movement in the 1970s that would itself capture the presidency in 1980. Indeed, one moderate educational journal, the *American School Board Journal,* would characterize the NEA-AFT philosophical movement in such terms "as the NEA radicalizes; the AFT is grabbing the center."[38]

The NEA leadership's decision to enter presidential politics was based on a sound rationale. Nationally, the president is the crucial political actor who not only creates the matrix for policy, but can place policy constraints through the judicious use of the veto. NEA leaders believe that their efforts in Congress could be undone through a presidential veto. More important, teacher influence with the president could present a stronger image for education.

The choice in 1976 for the teacher unions was equally clear. Democratic presidential candidates had made education a priority since Harry Truman. On the other hand, the Republican candidates had not perceived education as a vital national issue. Consequently, the teacher unions felt constrained to support the nominee of the Democratic party.

The 1976 presidential election was an unusual one: an unelected incumbent (Gerald Ford had been appointed vice president when Spiro Agnew resigned and had succeeded to the presidency when Richard Nixon resigned) versus a virtual unknown—Jimmy Carter, a former Georgia governor who had emerged from a large field of better-known candidates to attain the Democratic presidential nomination. At a time of public disenchantment with national politicians, Carter's rise can perhaps be attributed to his lack of connection to Washington and his emphasis on restoring trust in government.

The NEA settled on Carter at their annual convention in Miami after the two political conventions had chosen their nominees. The NEA leadership recommended Carter as the NEA candidate and mailed ballots to the 10,000 teacher delegates who had attended the union convention. The ballots listed four options: one for the Democratic candidate; one for the Republican candidate; one for a third party candidate; and one for "no endorsement."[39]

The NEA supported Carter mainly because of his declaration on education. Carter had promised to make education a "number one priority of the Federal government."[40] For the NEA, that priority first meant creating a separate Department of Education, and Carter agreed. The result was that such a department was eventually cre-

ated during the Carter tenure. Carter pursued the NEA endorsement as early as 1974 when he appeared at the NEA convention,
two years before the election, to seek support. It was a tactic that
brought dividends.

The NEA mobilized its considerable resources. The union established a goal of raising $1.5 million for its presidential canpaign
fund, in addition to the $4.5 million it had already for that pur-
pose.[41] And the NEA, according to one observer, was able to command some 500,000 teacher volunteers to campaign for its candidate.[42] It was such numbers that infuriated Republican and
conservative supporters. In the end, the 1976 presidential election
of Jimmy Carter was a high watermark in teacher politics.

The 1980 election was a different matter. The NEA decided early
to endorse its friend, President Jimmy Carter. A secret ballot was
held at the NEA's convention before the Democratic convention
voted to endorse Carter; a total of 77 percent of those NEA delegates voted for Carter.[43] On the other hand, the AFT proceeded
in another direction. Dissatisfied with the increasingly conservative policies of President Carter, the AFT, spurred by the leadership, chose to support Senator Edward Kennedy in the Democratic primary. One must conclude, however, that AFT President
Albert Shanker and his colleagues were equally motivated by a
desire to gain AFT influence—apart from the NEA—with a plau-
sible Democratic candidate.

AFT President Shanker's proclaimed reason for endorsing Kennedy was that President Carter had "changed."[44] Carter's declaration to balance the budget made him appear to be more like a
Republican in Shanker's estimation. "We don't want a Democratic
candidate," Shanker declared "running on a program which we ex-
pect from a conservative Republican."[45] On the other hand, for
Shanker and the AFT, Senator Kennedy had been "a champion for
health care, help for urban areas, gun control and many other issues which address human needs."[46] What was not mentioned in
this litany was Senator Kennedy's support of affirmative action programs and negotiations with the Soviet Union—positions anathema
to Shanker and the AFT.

By 1980, the scenario had changed for President Carter. Events
had made him vulnerable and Senator Kennedy posed a serious
threat to his renomination and election. For many, the president

was perceived as being ineffective on the domestic front; the nation was crippled with "stagflation"—both rising inflation and unemployment. On the foreign policy front, the Iranian revolution and ensuing hostage crisis proved to be the final blow to the Carter presidency. Although both the stagflation problem, resulting in large measure from high oil prices, and the Iran crisis could be attributed in part to the Middle East policies of previous administrations, the onus for these developments fell squarely on Carter.

Senator Kennedy, however, had deficits of his own. For one thing, he was attempting what Theodore White termed "from the beginning, historically preposterous . . . (seeking) . . . to destroy the chief of his own party."[47] Moreover, Kennedy's tragic Chappaquidick episode, and the questions it raised about the senator's character, had not been forgotten. AFT President Shanker would explain Kennedy's defeat in the primaries "because of some early stumbles, because of Chappaquidick, because of rallying around the flag during the hostage crisis."[48]

Nevertheless, Kennedy made a spirited attempt. Although he lost a crucial first primary in neighboring New Hampshire decisively (47.3 percent for Carter, to 37.3 percent for Kennedy), he rallied, winning such important states as New York, New Jersey, Connecticut, Pennsylvania and California.[49] The AFT was a prominent influence in Kennedy's victory in New York, Pennsylvania and Connecticut.[50]

The AFT sent 101 pro-Kennedy delegates to the 1980 Democratic Convention, but a fourth of those sent by the NEA for Carter.[51] By the end of the primaries, Carter had gained 1,971 delegates to Kennedy's 1,221—enough to pass the necessary 1,666 to win the nomination.[52] Kennedy had posed a serious challenge to Carter, sufficient to further damage Carter's re-election fortunes.

Still, the President had a chance. His Republican opponent, Ronald Reagan, former governor of California, was preceived as a hard-line conservative on the fringes of the Republican party. He had been handily defeated by President Ford in the 1976 Republican primaries; however, a third candidate entered the race—John Anderson, Republican Congressman of Illinois. After being defeated by Reagan in the Republican primary, Anderson ran as an independent. Voters who were fearful of Reagan's extreme conservatism, but disenchanted with Carter's inefficiency, would vote for Anderson. In the popular vote, Reagan had garnered 43,899,248 to Carter's 35,481,435 and Anderson's 5,719,437.[53] Reagan carried all but six states and the District of Columbia.

By 1984, the teachers unions were on the defensive. President Reagan had become a formidable candidate for re-election. Both the NEA and AFT decided to endorse a Democratic candidate in the primaries, and not wait until after the party's convention. The strategy was to support a winner early so as to maximize political resources. The AFT followed the lead of the AFL-CIO which had, for the first time, endorsed a primary candidate. According to the AFT, this was necessary since "only 59 percent of labor union members voted for Jimmy Carter so that Reagan's margin of victory was through blue-collar and labor votes that traditionally go to Democratic candidates."[54]

The choice of the NEA and the AFT was former Vice President Mondale. For the NEA, Mondale was an old friend of education, who many would have preferred over Carter in 1976. For the AFT, Mondale held a "lifetime AFT voting record of 98 percent" and had always "received the AFT's endorsement."[55] And for the AFL-CIO, Mondale had always allied with labor. In addition, the AFT conducted a poll at its 1983 annual convention, prior to the primaries, on viable candidates. Mondale was a big winner, with AFT members choosing him over Reagan 83 percent to 5 percent, with 12 percent undecided.[56] Other Democratic candidates did not fare as well. Senator John Glenn (D-Ohio) had a slimmer margin over Reagan: 67 percent to 5 percent, with 28 percent undecided.[57] Senator Gary Hart's (D-Colo.) percentage over Reagan was 63 percent to 6 percent, with 31 percent undecided.[58] In October 1983, the AFT leadership endorsed Mondale, and the NEA followed suit at the July 1984 convention.

Another reason for the two teacher unions (along with the AFL-CIO) to choose Mondale was the implicit anti-union campaign of the leading contender, Senator Gary Hart. Hart had campaigned on a "new ideas" approach, breeching the traditional liberalism of the Democratic party by opposing "big labor." Indeed, Hart accused Mondale of being a captive of "special interests" because of his "endorsement by the AFL-CIO and the two big teacher unions."[59]

The NEA ran a difficult course in endorsing Mondale. There was some sentiment at the convention for Hart and other candidates. What resulted was a political maneuver some observers considered a ploy to endorse Mondale. According to these critics within the NEA, the NEA leadership was "wary of provoking a floor fight during the Assembly that would show division and dilute the value of the endorsement."[60] Consequently, the leaders resorted to a mail ballot that had been replaced in the 1980 convention by a floor vote. According to the NEA critics, the delegates "once separated from one another . . . would be less likely to mount a challenge to the leadership's recommendation."[61] In the end, the NEA delegates endorsed Mondale by a mail vote.

In these three presidential scenarios, the teacher unions scored mixed results. In 1976, the teacher unions, and the NEA in particular, were instrumental in helping elect a virtual unknown, Governor Jimmy Carter, to the presidency. The attempt to repeat in 1980 failed; however, that loss was closer than it appeared at first glance.

But 1984 was different. President Reagan had become enormously popular. His economic policies contributed to prosperity, at least in the short term, and his foreign policy appeared decisive. Conservatism was the national mood. On the other hand, Vice President Mondale had inherited the legacy of his superior, President Carter, and that proved a burden too great to bear. The result was a staggering loss for the teacher unions.

How could the teacher unions be so successful in 1976, and fail in 1980 and 1984? The variables for a presidential election are extremely diffuse and complex. In the first case, the national issues favored the Democratic candidate and in the latter instances, they did not. A presidential election is, in effect, a referendum on national policies. Moreover, it would be foolhardy to suggest that the teacher unions, *alone,* despite their considerable resources, could sway such a national election. They may prove decisive in a close contest but 3.5 million teachers are but a part of the national electorate.

On the other hand, the teacher unions may have their greatest impact in choosing Presidential candidates in the primaries. Surely, the teacher unions have demonstrated great power in choosing the presidential candidates in the last Democratic primaries. In 1976, the NEA sent 265 delegates to the 1976 Democratic National Convention.[62] And the AFT sent more delegates than any other AFL-CIO union.[63] By 1980, the NEA sent 464 delegates and 169 alternates.[64] This caused one critic to observe that the NEA "constituted the most dominant special interest block ever to weave its wants into the fabric of a national party."[65] At the Oklahoma Democratic Convention, one observer pointed out that 43 percent of the delegates were teachers.[66] And at the 1980 Democratic National Convention, eleven NEA teachers were members of the party's platform committee.[67] By 1984, the NEA would send some 270 delegates to the Democratic convention.[68] In short, the teacher unions have displayed their greatest strength in the selection of a presidential nominee.

## THE LIMITS OF POWER

The political strength of the teacher unions has been established; however, this political power has limits. The NEA and the AFT are not always successful despite substantial financial and manpower resources. Moreover, the NEA and AFT may oppose one another in political campaigns, especially in the primaries.

Let us examine two case studies of congressional campaigns in 1986 that attracted national attention. First, there is the congressional campaign in the 8th District in the Boston area, where a Kennedy entered and won the race. Second, let us analyze the senatorial contest in Maryland where two women opposed each other for only the second time in history. Both case studies reveal how intricate the variables are in politics. In both cases, the NEA candidate was defeated in the Democratic Primaries, whereas the AFT candidate won, despite the NEA's superior resources.

The 1986 congressional elections signified a shift to the Democratic party. In the U.S. Senate, Democrats gained control from Republicans by majority of 55 to 45 seats.[69] In the House, already under Democratic control, the Democratic majority was slightly increased by one percentage point to 52 percent Democratic.[70] Despite the Democratic victory, the 1986 Congressional elections, in presidential mid-term, were widely viewed as contests "with few nationwide themes," with an "enormously popular" president but with an absence of "international crisis or sharp domestic controversy."[71] As a result, voter turnout was estimated to be its lowest since 1942—37.3 percent—and the third lowest in U.S. history.[72] Still, this did not preclude the election from being "the most expensive Congressional campaign in the nation's history."[73] The Federal Elections Committee reported that a total of $342 million was spent on the congressional campaigns, $80 million more than in 1984.[74] This was further testimony of how a combination of PACs and television campaigning were changing American politics.

The NEA had achieved a significant measure of success in the 1986 congressional elections. The NEA had endorsed twenty-eight Democrats and one Republican in the Senate races. Of these, nine NEA incumbent candidates won and one lost. Of the challengers, five NEA-suported candidates won, and seven lost, and of the open seats, five-NEA backed candidates won, and two lost. In total, nineteen NEA-backed Senate candidates won, and ten lost, making a 66 percent win.[75]

In the House of Representatives, the NEA scored a more impressive victory. The NEA supported 291 Democrats and 19 Republicans. Of the incumbents endorsed by NEA, 224 won, and one lost. Of the challengers supported by the NEA, 5 won, and 47 lost. Of the open seats, 21 NEA-backed candidates won, and 11 lost. In total, 250 NEA supported candidates won, and 59 lost, making an 81 percent win in the House. Totally in both Senate and House races, the overall winning percentage for the NEA was 80 percent.[76]

### Case Study: The Kennedy Contest

Perhaps the best illustration of the limits of teacher union power was the election of Joseph Kennedy II to Congress. The NEA failed to endorse young Kennedy, the oldest son of former Senator and presidential aspirant Robert Kennedy, in the Democratic primary for the 8th Congressional District in Massachusetts. This district was considered one of the key Democratic strongholds in the nation. Defying the political establishment that endorsed Kennedy, the NEA, for complex reasons, chose to endorse a far more liberal—and considered a more competent—candidate, State Senator George Bachrach. Despite the "magic" of the Kennedy name,

Bachrach and the NEA made a run of it until Kennedy prevailed in a close primary election, and, eventually in the November election.

The 8th Congressional District is a composite of the main constituency of the Democratic party: affluent liberals, mostly connected with the universities, and a sizeable working class. The latter is composed of ethnic groups such as the Irish, the Italian and Armenians. The district is comprised of parts of Boston, Cambridge, Belmont, Watertown, Arlington and Waltham. Of the 522,000 registered voters, 62 percent are Democrats, and only 9 percent are Republicans.[77] In 1984, only 36 percent of the district voters chose Ronald Reagan, one of the lowest tallies for the president in the nation.[78] The 8th Congressional District was the one from which President John F. Kennedy, uncle of Joseph Kennedy II, began his political career. Thomas P. (Tip) O'Neill, House Speaker, succeeded Kennedy and retained the post until his retirement in 1986. In addition to being represented by President Kennedy, Massachusetts has been represented by Senator Edward Kennedy, a presidential candidate and a national political figure. In sum, Joseph Kennedy II, is related to three presidential candidates, all born in Massachusetts. In addition, John Kennedy's maternal grandfather John J. "Honey Fitz" Fitzgerald had long been mayor in Boston. The combination was powerful. The Kennedy dynasty in Massachusetts politics has been akin to other family dynasties such as the Longs in Louisiana.

Nevertheless, there were nine Democratic candidates vying to succeed House Speaker O'Neill. In addition to Kennedy, there were three other major candidates, the most formidable being State Senator George Bachrach. Bachrach had gained a reputation as a "maverick reformer" in the state senate.[79] Another major candidate was the grandson of former President Franklin D. Roosevelt. And finally, Melvin H. King was another serious candidate. King had previously made a strong challenge in the Boston mayoral election and was considered "probably the most popular black politician in Massachusetts and a widely respected civil rights leader."[80]

Of the nine candidates, the thirty-three-year-old Kennedy was, perhaps, the least accomplished. Although graduating from the University of Massachusetts at Boston, he had a checkered academic career. Kennedy transferred from two prepatory schools and three colleges.[81] Moreover, he carried the Kennedy "curse" as well as the "magic." In 1973, he was convicted of reckless driving in an accident that left a girl paralyzed.[82] This accident had evoked the Chappaquidick incident involving his uncle, Senator Ted Kennedy.

Most important, young Kennedy had little political experience. His only public service experience was as the head of a private non-profit agency—Citizens Energy—formed in 1979 to aid low income citizens with their heating bills. And in televised debates, Kennedy was often inept and lacked political sophistication. He appeared the least capable of the nine Democratic candidates.[83]

Nevertheless, there was the "magic" of the Kennedy name. As cited, that name invoked one president, two presidential contenders, and a mayor of Boston. Consequently, the Massachusetts political establishment felt more comfortable in endorsing young Kennedy. He received the support of retiring House Speaker O'Neill, Boston Mayor Raymond L. Flynn, and the liberal Boston *Globe* and the conservative Boston *Herald*.[84] Moreover, Kennedy had national support from political leaders. For example, two of the nation's most prominent black leaders, Atlanta Mayor Andrew Young and Coretta Scott King, sponsored a $100-a-person cocktail party to raise money for Kennedy.[85]

Kennedy's chief challenger, George Bachrach, possessed impressive credentials. Also a young 34, Bachrach was a graduate of Trinity College and Boston University Law School.[86] He had been a state senator since 1981. He was known as a liberal, receiving a 100 percent rating from the Americans for Democratic Action.[87] Moreover, the Massachusetts affiliate of the NEA had rated Bachrach 94 percent for his support of education in the state senate.[88] An independent thinker, he was known to challenge the Democratic leadership in the legislature on occasion.

The Massachusetts Teachers Association, the NEA affiliate, endorsed Bachrach. MTA president Nancy Finkelstein was effusive, citing Bachrach's education record and overwhelmingly liberal credentials. On the other hand, the Boston Federation of Teachers (BPT), the AFT affiliate, endorsed Kennedy. Although the total membership of the BFT was only 12,000, in contrast to the MTA's 61,000, most of the BFT's members were located in the 8th Congressional District, whereas the MTA had only about 5,000 members there. As a result, the Boston Federation of Teachers may have had a greater impact on the election.

The campaign had added national importance as a microcosm of the conflicting ideological trends in the Democratic party. The race was perceived nationally as a contest between the "Democratic Party's longtime base among the working class ethnics and its liberal component"—between ethnic Boston and university liberals.[89] Kennedy was the candidate of the former group whereas Bachrach was the champion of the latter. Kennedy tailored his issues to appeal to the working class, the elderly, and the poor. On the other hand, Bachrach played to the affluent young urban professionals.

Among Kennedy's centrist positions was favoring the death penalty. One observer remarked that Kennedy adopted the position on the death penalty as "a concession to his working class supporters."[90] In addition he favored aiding the Contra rebels seeking to overthrow the leftist Sandinista regime in Nicaragua. He "reluctantly" approved abortion.[91] Kennedy's cautious centrist politics prompted Melvin King, the black activist candidate, to charge that Kennedy's positions were "closer to Ronald Reagan's."[92]

By contrast, Bachrach concentrated on purely "liberal" issues. He made arms control and opposition to the United States financing a questionable rebellion in Nicaragua central issues. Bachrach labeled Kennedy as "the candidate of the right."[93] Bachrach displayed superior skills in debate, revealing a solid grasp of issues and a keen intelligence.[94] However, he clearly lacked charisma—a handicap in a race against the Kennedy "magic."

Why did Kennedy win? Clearly the inferior candidate of the nine, Kennedy had large political deficits. His election indicates the volatility of political variables. First Kennedy possessed the larger resources. He spent over $1 million, more than double that of his closest rival, Bachrach.[95] Second, his family connections brought him support from the Democratic establishment both in Massachusetts and nationally. Of the support of the two teacher organizations, he may have had the more crucial one in terms of members in his district. And finally, the most important, he had the Kennedy name. In Massachusetts, that alone is tantamount to success.

On the other hand, why did the NEA choose to support Bachrach? First, the NEA's support was a matter of loyalty to a proven friend and sound politics. One NEA national official explained that the "MTA had a debt to Bachrach, and it's just good politics in the long run to stick with your friends in education, otherwise you will lose credibility."[96] Second, Bachrach's more liberal positions on the issues were more closely aligned to the NEA's. (This association is true also in the following case study set in Maryland.) Third, the NEA fully believed that Bachrach had an excellent chance of winning. This was indicated in the closeness of the polls prior to the primary election. In the end, the NEA showed loyalty, independence and an ability not to be intimidated by even the strongest of political candidates.

### Case Study: Barnes-Mikulski-Chavez Contest

Another nationally significant contest in the 1986 congressional elections was for the U.S. Senate in Maryland. In that race, the scenario presumed that a long-term popular centrist Democrat, Congresswoman Barbara Mikulski, would oppose a former Republican Reagan aide, Linda Chavez. It would be only the second time in U.S. history that two women opposed one another in a senatorial contest. The previous time had occurred in Maine twenty-six years before.[97] After a decade and a half of the women's movement, such a contest held singular national interest. In the end, Congresswoman Mikulski prevailed over seven Democratic primary rivals and Republican candidate Chavez.

Again, however, the NEA supported an unsuccessful candidate. The NEA endorsed Congressman Michael Barnes, a liberal Democrat. On the other hand, the AFT affiliate in Baltimore, the Baltimore Teachers Union, endorsed Mikulski. The Maryland State Teachers Association (the MSTA of the NEA) was the dominant organization with 33,000 members statewide, whereas the Baltimore Teacher's Union had only 6,000 members.[98] Nevertheless, Baltimore accounts for 60 percent of registered Democrats in Democratic primaries and was Mikulski's home city.[99] Still, the contested office was a statewide office.

The MSTA chose Barnes purely on educational grounds. Both Barnes and Mikulski had similar liberal voting records in the House. Of forty key votes surveyed by the Congressional Quarterly between 1979 through 1985, the two differed only five times.[100] However, the turning point for the MSTA was tuition tax credits.

Barnes opposed them and Mikulski favored them. Since the NEA was adamantly opposed to tuition tax credits (as was the AFT), the MSTA decided to support Barnes. Parenthetically, one wonders why the Baltimore Teachers Union would not refrain from supporting Mikulski on the same grounds.

In addition, Barnes had registered a 100 percent NEA voting record for his last three terms in Congress.[101] MSTA political contact members would report that, on educational issues, Barnes "always espoused the same position held by the Association."[102] He voted consistently against cuts in education spending. Most important, he supported the NEA's chief project, the creation of a U.S. Department of Education. MSTA President Beverly L. Corelle would term Barnes a "true friend of public education and public educators."[103]

Equally important, Barnes' liberal political ideology was more congenial to the NEA. One observer described him as "a 'golden boy' in the House who has achieved national publicity for his opposition to the Reagan Administration's Central American Policy."[104] And once again the Barnes-Mikulski contest reflected the deepening divisions within the Democratic party's constituency. Like the Kennedy-Bachrach contest, Mikulski appealed to the traditional ethnic and working-class interests, whereas Barnes appealed to affluent liberal professionals. Barnes' residence and constituency was affluent Montgomery County, a suburb of Washington, D.C. It was a constituency described by a longtime Barnes supporter as "more the wine and cheese set."[105] By contrast, Mikulski, who is of Polish extraction, had her roots in ethnic working-class Baltimore. Mikulski displayed statewide strength as well and by August was well ahead of her six other challengers and led Barnes by 45 percent to 21 percent in the polls.[106]

The MSTA was well aware of the uphill struggle to elect Barnes in the primary—an election that was tantamount to victory in generally Democratic Maryland. MSTA President Beverly L. Corelle outlined the scenario:

Whenever we discuss political endorsements, the question of electability always arises. Mike Barnes is definitely moving up in the polls. His name is achieving more and more recognition. With our support for his campaign, he can win that office. As more and more Marylanders hear him and his message, we can bring even greater support to him. If we have a chance to make a difference in a political race, it is here.[107]

Barnes did improve his chances, but not enough. In the seven person race, he garnered 29 percent of the vote with Mikulski receiving a dominant 53 percent.[108]

The November election had another interest. The Republican candidate, Linda Chavez, was formerly an education editor on the national staff of the AFT. Her articles on the teaching of traditional values attracted the attention of the head of the National Endowment for the Humanities, William Bennett. Bennett, who subsequently became Secretary of the Department of Education, persuaded Chavez to become a member of the U.S. Commission on Civil Rights.[109]

Chavez was originally a native of New Mexico from a Hispanic family who traversed the political spectrum. She began as a young Socialist in the 1970s, belonging to the Young People's Socialist League, the youth arm of the more mainstream Socialist party.[110] By the eighties she had converted to Reagan conservatism. Although proclaiming the value of the work ethic, she defaulted on thousands of dollars of student loans until a decade after college when she was traced as a federal employee.[111]

Linda Chavez was appointed staff director of the Reagan administration's reconstituted U.S. Civil Rights Commission. The Reagan commission became an advocate against affirmative action. Chavez was credited along with other Reagan appointees as redirecting the commission "on a variety of controversial civil rights matters including taking a position against the use of numerical goals to remedy the effects of past discrimination."[112] Her position against affirmative action programs was clear. She informed an interviewer from the *Washington Post* that "the problems facing minorities today, and Blacks in particular, cannot be solved by civil rights laws."[113]

Her role on the commission resulted in her emerging "as a favorite of conservatives, who waged a campaign for her appointment to the White House where she became Chief of the White House Liaison Office"—a position the *New York Times* believed provided her with "more opportunity to influence policy."[114]

Chavez was described in an interview with the *New York Times* as a former Democrat who eventually switched to the Republican party in 1980 with the advent of Ronald Reagan. She characterized herself as one who "became strongly anti-communist" and "was critical in her college days of the movement that opposed the Vietnam War."[115] She refused to vote in 1972 and 1976 because she feared the Democratic presidential candidates would weaken the military and by 1980 became a Reagan "devotee," "impressed with conservative positions on foreign and military policies."[116]

Chavez attempted to portray the election as a choice between liberalism and conservatism. President Reagan campaigned for her. Chavez branded Mikulski as a "San Francisco-style, George McGovern liberal" attempting to invoke the implication of the large homosexual community in that city and McGovern's strong liberalism.[117] She charged that Mikulski had once hired a radical feminist on her staff who, according to Chavez, held "anticapitalist, Marxist views."[118]

Nevertheless, it was an uphill battle for Chavez. In a heavily Democratic state with a popular five-term congresswoman, Chavez had little chance. Moreover, Mikulski had more money, collecting $1,428,142 by September 30 to Chavez's $737,105.[119] Mikulski won handily.

In summary, the teacher unions exercise considerable power and influence in school board elections, local, state, and national political elections—including the presidency. Still, there are limits to that power. The teacher unions are constrained in their support. First there is the matter of educational philosophy. The teacher unions must endorse only those candidates who most support their educational goals. In addition, there is political ideology. As we shall see in greater detail in the following chapter, the two teacher unions consider issues beyond the educational realm, from social policy to foreign policy. In these matters, the NEA and AFT differ slightly but significantly. And finally, there are intangibles. As in the Kennedy case, political appeal to the voters may transcend rational qualifications and support. Still, on balance, the teacher unions are formidable political actors.

## NOTES

1. Marilyn Gittell, with Maurice R. Berube et al., *School Decentralization and School Policy in New York City* (New York: Institute for Community Studies, 1971), p. 41.

2. Ibid., p. 29.

3. Ibid.

4. Ibid., p. 28.

5. Marilyn Gittell, with Maurice R. Berube et al., *School Boards and School Policy* (New York: Praeger, 1973), p. 10.

6. Gittell with Berube et al., *School Decentralization and School Policy in New York City*, p. 41.

7. Gittell with Berube et al., *School Boards and School Policy*, p. 10.

8. Ibid.

9. Ibid.

10. Judith Baum, Director of Information Services, Public Education Association, "Community School Board Elections: Candidates List," May 6, 1986 (data analyzed and tabulated by the author.

11. Ibid.

12. Ibid.

13. *New York Times*, December 17, 1986, p. 32.

14. Ibid.

15. *New York Teacher*, September 29, 1986, pp. 6-7.

16. Ibid., p. 2A.

17. Ibid., p. 6.

18. Ibid.

19. Ibid.

20. Ibid.; *New York Times*, November 5, 1986, p. B14 (data analyzed and tabulated by the author).

21. *New York Teacher*, September 29, 1986, p. 6; *New York Times*, November 6, 1986, p. B15 (data analyzed and tabulated by the author).

22. *New York Teacher*, September 1, 1986, p. 6.

23. *New York Times*, January 25, 1987, p. 18.

24. *New York Times*, May 25, 1986, p. E6.

25. *New York Times*, October 28, 1986, p. B1.

26. *New York Teacher*, September 1, 1986, p. 6.

27. Ibid.

28. Scott Jaschik, "On New York Campuses, Cuomo Draws Strong Support, Vociferous Criticism," *Chronicle of Higher Education*, September 17, 1986, p. 22.

29. Ibid.

30. R. W. Apple, Jr., "The Question of Mario Cuomo," *New    York Times Magazine*, September 14, 1986, p. 46.

31. *New York Times*, October 25, 1986, p. 31.

32. Ibid.

33. *New York Times*, October 27, 1986, p. B1.

34. Apple, "The Question of Mario Cuomo," p. 87.

35. *New York Times*, November 20, 1986, p. 1.

36. Ibid.

37. Apple, "The Question of Mario Cuomo," p. 48.

38. "What the Teacher Unions Have in Store for You," *American School Board Journal*, September 1975, p. 38.

39. Ibid., p. 34.

40. J. D. Heisner, "Teachers Helped Put Them There; Now Carter and Mondale Are Accountable, Too," *Instructor*, January 1977, p. 135.

41. *London Times Educational Supplement*, January 9, 1976, p. 14.

42. George Neill, "NEA: New Powerhouse in the Democratic Party," *Phi Delta Kappan*, October 1980, p. 85.

43. "N.E.A. and A.F.T. Put Their Power on the Line for Carter," *American School Board Journal*, November 1980, p. 30.

44. Albert Shanker, "If You Love New York, Vote for Kennedy," *New York Times*, March 23, 1980, p. E9.

45. Ibid.

46. Ibid.

47. Theodore A. White, *America in Search of Itself: The Making of the President, 1956–1980* (New York: Harper and Row, 1982), p. 275.

48. Albert Shanker, "No, I'm Not Sorry I Supported Kennedy," *New York Times*, August 17, 1980, p. E9.

49. White, *America in Search of Itself*, p. 297.

50. Challenge of the 1980s: A Political Report," *American Teacher*, September 1980, p. 7.

51. Ibid.

52. White, *America in Search of Itself*, p. 302.

53. Ibid., pp. 435-36.

54. *American Teacher*, December 1983/January 1984, p. 9.

55. Ibid.

56. Ibid.

57. Ibid.

58. Ibid.

59. Albert Shanker, "Mondale Is the Right Choice," *American Teacher*, May 1984, p. 5.

60. Bill Boyton and John Lloyd, "Why the Largest Teachers Union

Puts Its Staff First and Education Second," *Washington Monthly*, May 1985, p. 29.

61. Ibid.

62. Eugene H. Methvin, "The NEA: A Washington Lobby Run Rampant," *Reader's Digest*, November 1978, p. 97.

63. Albert Shanker, "Education and Politics: Emerging Alliances," *Educational Leadership*, November 1976, p. 137.

64. White, *America in Search of Itself*, p. 334.

65. Eugene H. Methvin, "Guess Who Spells Disaster for Education?" *Reader's Digest*, May 1984, p. 91.

66. Jerome Cramer, "Here's How Teacher Power Affects You," *American School Board Journal*, November 1980, p. 36.

67. Ibid, p. 35.

68. *London Times Education Supplement*, July 13, 1984, p. 14.

69. *New York Times*, November 6, 1986, p. A1.

70. Ibid., p. A29.

71. *New York Times*, August 31, 1986, p. A1.

72. *New York Times*, November 8, 1986, p. 8.

73. *New York Times*, November 7, 1986, p. A19.

74. Ibid.

75. National Education Association Memorandum, NEA-PAC Endorsement-Election Report: 1986 Election Cycle, Washington, D.C., November 11, 1986.

76. Ibid.

77. George V. Higgins, "Challenging the Kennedy 'Magic,' " *New York Times Magazine*, August 3, 1986, p. 18.

78. Ibid.

79. Ibid, p. 22.

80. *New York Times*, August 18, 1986, p. A8.

81. *New York Times*, September 16, 1986, p. A12.

82. Ibid.

83. League of Women Voters, "The 8th Congressional Primary Election Debate," Boston, Mass., *C-SPAN* (Television), September 2, 1986.

84. *New York Times*, September 16, 1986, p. A12.

85. *New York Times*, August 18, 1986, p. A8.

86. Higgins, "Challenging the Kennedy 'Magic,' " p. 22.

87. *New York Times*, August 18, 1986, p. A8.

88. Telephone interview with Guessippina Bonner, Political Specialist, Massachusetts Teachers Association, Boston, Mass., August 28, 1986.

89. *New York Times*, September 16, 1986, p. A12.

90. Ibid.

91. Ibid.

92. *New York Times*, August 18, 1986, p. A8.

93. Ibid.

94. League of Women Voters, "The 8th Congressional Primary Election Debate."

95. *New York Times*, September 16, 1986, p. A12.

96. Telephone interview with Joseph Standa, Political Specialist, National Education Association, Washington, D.C., October 20, 1986.

97. *New York Times*, August 31, 1986, p. 58.

98. Telephone interview with Kathleen Lyons, Political Specialist, Maryland State Teachers Association, Baltimore, Md., September 3, 1986.

99. *New York Times*, September 10, 1986, p. A15.

100. *New York Times*, August 31, 1986, p. 50.

101. Beverly L. Corelle, President, Maryland State Teachers Association, "1986 Representative Assembly Recommends Michael Barnes for U.S. Senate" (Press Release), Baltimore, Md., April 19, 1986, p. 1.

102. Ibid, p. 2.

103. Ibid, p. 3.

104. *New York Times*, August 31, 1986, p. 58.

105. Ibid.

106. Ibid.

107. Corelle, "1986 Representative Assembly Recommends Michael Barnes for U.S. Senate," p. 3.

108. *Washington Post*, September 11, 1986, p. A24.

109. *Washington Post*, October 29, 1986, p. A12.

110. Ibid.

111. Ibid.

112. *New York Times*, June 3, 1985, p. A16.

113. *Washington Post*, October 29, 1986, p. A12.

114. *New York Times*, June 3, 1985, p. A16.

115. Ibid.

116. Ibid.

117. *Washington Post*, September 11, 1986, p. A1.

118. *Washington Post*, October 29, 1986, p. A12.

119. *New York Times*, October 17, 1986, p. A18.

# 5

# The NEA vs. the AFT:
# Is There a Difference?

The question arises whether the two teacher unions differ on fundamental educational and social issues. The answer seems to be that, for the most part, they do. On a range of key educational and social items, the NEA and AFT differ significantly, with the former pursuing goals and strategies that are more politically and educationally liberal, and the latter those that are more conservative.

Differences have characterized the two organizations historically; however, these have become even sharper in recent years. Ironically, it is the once staid NEA that has become the more liberal of the two organizations and the radical upstart AFT, with its Socialist beginnings, the more conservative. During the 1960s, the two organizations appeared to have a great deal in common, both educationally and socially. The divergence was heightened with the ascensions of Albert Shanker as president of the AFT in 1974 and with Terry Herndon as executive director of the NEA in 1973 (until 1983).

We shall examine crucial issues that have emerged in the recent past on education, race and social matters and foreign policy. These controversies will serve to focus on the differing organizational styles of the two unions and the political means to accomplish differing objectives.

## EDUCATION

In education, the NEA and AFT differ on some important issues but agree on matters that severely threaten the existence of public schooling. The two rival unions disagree on a separate Department of Education, and bilingual education. There is some agreement on competency tests for teachers, in varying measure of support. However, both teacher organizations are strongly opposed to both a voucher plan and tuition tax credits, which have a potential to undermine public education and favor private schooling.

### Department of Education

There has been a difference between the NEA and AFT on the role of the federal government. During the 1970s, NEA officials publicly proclaimed that a crucial educational goal was to substantially increase the financial contribution of the federal government to public schools. For most of that decade, the federal share of public education hovered around 8 percent; the NEA wanted a dramatic increase to a full third of the costs of public education. The reasoning was that public education was a national concern that demanded national strategies and resources. On the other hand, AFT officials had not thought through the federal issue and refrained from comment.

One side issue of the NEA's push for a larger federal role, however, was that of creating a separate Department of Education. Since its formation in 1869, the Office of Education has been mandated mainly to collect educational statistics. However, as the federal role expanded, somewhat surreptitiously, and especially with the school reform movement of the 1960s, the Office of Education gained in influence.

NEA officials hoped that a separate Department of Education would confer official status to education as a symbol of national concern. Moreover, it would be a step in the direction to a more coordinated, less decentralized, educational system. It was argued by NEA proponents that the United States was the only nation, both in the democratic and communist worlds, without a national department of education. The NEA made a separate Department of Education a priority political item. The AFT decided to oppose it.

NEA's support of Governor Jimmy Carter in 1976 was partly predicated on its candidate creating a separate education department. On the other hand, the AFT had initially supported Senator Ted Kennedy in the Democratic primaries, and was cool to the idea. AFT President Albert Shanker devoted two columns in the *New York Times* denouncing a separate education department. He argued that creating such a department merely for "prestige" was "not a good reason" since it would build another bureaucratic layer in education.[1] Shanker was joined in opposition to the concept by AFL-CIO President George Meany among others.

In 1979, President Carter created a Department of Education. In his campaign for the presidency in 1980, Governor Ronald Reagan pledged to abolish the separate cabinent department. Indeed, his first Secretary of Education, Terrence Bell, fully recommended such a move. However, the emergence of the "excellence" school reform movement in 1983 made President Reagan table that campaign pledge. Education had become a 1984 campaign issue, and Reagan was sufficiently astute to perceive the political gain in maintaining the status quo.

### Bilingual Education

Another area of disagreement over educational issues was that of bilingual education. Since 1969, the federal government had sponsored educational programs whereby students are first instructed in their native language and then a transition is made to English. The federal government established a Bilingual Education Act and in 1974 the Supreme Court in the *Lau* decision upheld the concept. The NEA supports this version of bilingual education whereas the AFT does not.

Critics of these bilingual programs charge that they are not effective. Proponents have argued that such programs constitute the best method to acculturate children of immigrants. The research evidence appears to be divided on the issue. Critics argue that students from another culture should be exposed only to English. Both the AFT and the Reagan administration comprise the major critics of bilingual education.

AFT President Shanker endorsed the Reagan proposal to dilute the original bilingual concept. Secretary of Education Bennett suggested that school districts be given an option to acculturate immigrant children with a "program of total immersion in English" rather than the dual language–method of the original program.[2] Bennett charged that the current programs mainly create cultural pride rather than teach English effectively.

### Competency Tests for Teachers

One of the more controversial issues of the reforms for "excellence" of the 1980s has been competency tests for teachers. Under this plan, states ordered both new and existing teachers to take competency tests in order to obtain or keep jobs. Both the AFT and the NEA—the latter reluctantly—endorsed the concept of tests for new teachers but opposed competency tests for current teachers.

Teacher competency tests are not new. Approximately 25 states have required National Teacher Examinations (NTE) as a condition of employment, in addition to requiring attendance at accredited colleges and universities. In one instance, NTE scores were used to enable black teachers to be considered for higher salaries in southern states in order to compete favorably with salaries of white teachers; the Supreme Court struck down the practice.[3] In 1983, 90 percent of the public polled by Gallup were strongly in favor of competency tests.[4] It is an issue of educational quality that is readily grasped by the public.

Initially, the teacher unions were defensive. But in 1985 AFT President Shanker made a dramatic turnaround, calling for a national licensing examination system. Six months later, the NEA would echo the demand for testing prospective teachers.

One problem with competency tests was their effect on black teachers. Black teachers scored lower on NTE examinations. In recent years that trend continued with competency tests. In Arizona, 66 percent of minorities failed the tests; in Georgia, 40 percent; in California, 42 percent.[5] There was a fear among black educators that competency tests would severely deplete the ranks of black teachers, and concomitantly, provide fewer role models for black children. This fear was partly responsible for the NEA's hesitancy to endorse any form of testing. On the other hand, the AFT's Shanker saw no real concern. What was needed, he claimed, was to "provide intensive help to promising minority and other low income students."[6]

Other observers expressed deep concern. In Louisiana, for example, only 10 percent of black graduates passed the NTE. One educator predicted that extensive testing would spell doom for the teacher education programs at predominantly black universities.[7]

The heart of the matter, so far as the teacher unions were concerned, was the testing of experienced teachers. In 1985, Arkansas became the first state to mandate statewide competency tests for all teachers. Commenting on the Arkansas plan, Shanker termed the plan a "hoax" that changes "the rules in mid-game."[8] He countered that school board members, principals and other school administrators be also required to take competency tests. A year later in Texas, however, 96.7 percent of over 200,000 teachers passed the competency tests on their first try with a second attempt permitted in order to keep their jobs.[9]

The "excellence" school reform movement received a boost on the issue of testing when the prestigious Carnegie Foundation decided to create a national certification system for teachers. In a report entitled, *A Nation Prepared,* composed by fourteen leaders from education, business and science, the Carnegie Foundation proposed establishing a new National Board for Professional Teaching Standards. The proposed certification board would be established in June 1987, and would certify new teachers. This voluntary board would issue differentiated credentials—a Teaching Certificate for beginning teachers and an Advanced Teaching Certificate for those with superior skills.

Both AFT President Shanker and NEA President Mary Futrell served on the Carnegie study commission. And both had different views toward the report. Shanker was uncritical, calling the Carnegie plan "the first major move toward professionalism in teaching."[10] On the other hand, NEA President Futrell issued "a statement of support with reservations."[11] She preferred strengthening state standards boards and opposed the market approach of the commission to seek out educational entrepreneurs. She also took the occasion to lash out at the thrust of the reform movement for "excellence":

The Carnegie Task Force report solidly repudiates much of the nonsense that has passed for education "reform" over the past three years. Would-be reformers have argued, for instance, that schools are devoting too many resources to educating disadvantaged learners and not enough to fostering excellence among talented students.[12]

Concern for professional quality had spread to other professions. In May 1986, New York Governor Mario Cuomo, as a potential presidential candidate, proposed competency tests for all doctors. This was strikingly ironic, since the educational proponents of tests, Shanker among them, had used the medical profession as a model for teacher professionalism.

### Vouchers

One educational issue upon which both the NEA and AFT could agree was that of vouchers. Both organizations were adamant over the introduction of educational vouchers.

This is how a voucher plan would work. The federal government would assume the costs of education by issuing a financial chit, a voucher, to a parent. That parent would pay for the cost of school-ing at the school of his or her choice—either a public, private or parochial school. This would introduce choice to education, pro-ponents argue, and restore the law of the marketplace—competi-tion—to the monopoly of public education. Under this theory, those schools that are effective in educating students would attract more students, whereas least successful schools would go under.

Vouchers have had a curious history in the United States. Some European countries have implemented voucher plans in the early twentieth century, but the United States has yet to embark on such a course. In the United States, the voucher concept received its first serious consideration when it was introduced by the con-servative Nobel economist Milton Friedman. Later it was en-dorsed by the socialist educational sociologist Christopher Jencks. Jencks persuaded the poverty program officals in 1970 to conduct a pilot program in Alum Rock, California, for public schools only during the early 1970s. Vouchers were supported in the mid-1970s by the liberal educational finance reformer John Coons. Coons perceived a method whereby educational finances could be evenly distributed, and thus replace the controversial finance systems based on unequal property taxes. Finally, conservative educators within the Reagan administration seized on vouchers as the means by which to create educational competition.

The voucher plan was first tried on an experimental basis in the early 1970s. The Harvard educational sociologist Jencks proposed a modified version to the Office of Economic Opportunity (OEO), the old poverty program. OEO accepted and initiated a five-year, five-million-dollar experiment. Open bids from thirty pre-selected cities were encouraged. In an era of rising black city politics, Jencks and OEO officials finally chose Alum Rock, a suburb of San Diego, as their voucher city—a safe, if somewhat sanitized, choice. Critics wondered whether the experiment in Alum Rock could be generalized to any American cities.

Jencks modified his voucher plan in Alum Rock to include only public schools. Nevertheless, in his search for the ideal city, he seemed overly concerned about public support. He directed his associates to give serious consideration only to those cities that had "the strongest possible language in support of a voucher experiment . . . (from) teachers' union, mayor's office, Catholic school system, the non-public schools, key state legislators, governor's office, civil rights groups, community action agency, model city agency and, last, but certainly not least, parents groups."[13] Such a consensus, some critics felt, in an adversial democratic society, may only be reached in heaven. In the end, the Alum Rock experiment was inconclusive as to its educational effect.[14]

By the mid-1970s, the voucher plan took another turn. Educator Mario Fantini, an "old reformer" of the sixties identified with the community control movement, reformulated the Jencks modification of vouchers only for public schools. In his book *Public Schools of Choice*, Fantini argued that vouchers should be considered only within the framework of public schools. In this respect, vouchers, he contended, would have a positive effect of creating variety within the public education system without undermining its very foundation.

By the 1980s another variation emerged. Psychologist, attorney and educator, Barbara Lerner employed the concept for the poor. In her book, *Minimum Competence, Maximum Choice*, Lerner outlined a plan to have "vouchers for literacy." Vouchers would be given to a family with an illiterate child so that the child could attend a private school. A definition of illiteracy was to be determined by local standards of minimum competence for three years consecutively.

A number of politically conservative educators had advocated vouchers during the 1970s with the election of Ronald Reagan and the ushering in of a conservative age. Many top policy advisors in the Reagan government, including the president, had placed vouchers on a priority list. However, enormous budget deficits seemed to preclude the possibility of a large-scale voucher plan launched by the federal government. Nevertheless, the Reagan government adopted a version of the Lerner plan. In 1986, Secretary of Education William Bennett proposed legislation to Congress that would give Chapter I money for educating the poor in the form of vouchers to be spent at private and parochial schools. The suggested amount was $600 to each poor child served by Chapter I programs.

Nevertheless, the voucher plan had powerful enemies. In 1970, the AFT would brand the voucher plan as "hucksterism" that "could turn into a very costly and tragic mistake with farreaching social implications."[15] The American Jewish Congress would follow suit by terming the plan a "disaster for our country," fearing a breakdown of church-state separation.[16] And the National Association for the Advancement of Colored People cautioned against vouchers as promoting racial separation.[17]

In the 1980s, both the NEA and the AFT were strongly opposed to voucher plans that would encompass private and parochial schooling. However, by 1985, AFT President Shanker would amend his opposition to vouchers and endorse the Fantini concept of vouchers for public schools. The AFT and NEA based their opposition against vouchers on grounds of both altruism and self-interest. At best, they feared that vouchers would seriously undermine the very nature of public education in America. They also feared the diminution of teacher unionism under a fragmented, balkanized national voucher system.

Shanker cited the example of Holland with a voucher plan that destroyed public education in that country. Introduced in 1917, vouchers transformed the public school system from one educating 75 percent of the primary school population to one that today only accounts for 27 percent of elementary school youngsters.[18] In addition, Shanker criticized the Reagan plan of Chapter I vouchers on the grounds that private schools might "discriminate along racial or religious lines" and may eventually "pit one group of parents against another."[19]

NEA President Mary Futrell would call the Reagan plan a "cruel hoax" for the poor that "signals further retreat" from successfully educating the poor.[20] She alluded to the educational progress that has been made with Chapter I programs in recent years and warned about discarding a successful approach with an untried one. Moreover, NEA secretary-treasurer Roxanne Brastar would fear that the Reagan plan might create a two-tracked segregated school system that raised the "frightening specter of a return to segregated schools . . . and the eventual demise of our system of universal public education."[21]

Finally after much protest, Secretary of Education Bennett withdrew the voucher bill in the summer of 1986. It was a large success for the teacher unions; however, the next year the Reagan administration reintroduced the voucher plan in legislation for remedial education classes.

### Tuition Tax Credits

Closely linked to vouchers was the issue of tuition tax credits. The idea of tuition tax credits is to allow parents a tax credit for monies spent on either a parochial or private education for their youngsters. Again the NEA and AFT joined in opposition, whereas the Reagan administration and some key Democrats, such as Senator Daniel Moynihan of New York, supported legislation to enact tuition tax credits.

Proponents of tuition tax credits, such as the Catholic Church, with the largest parochial school system, contend that parochial school parents pay double for their child's education. That is, they pay the taxes that finance public schooling, and they pay again for their child's private schooling. On the other hand, critics of tuition tax credits argue that the concept would undermine public education. NEA and AFT officials do not oppose the right of a parent to have an alternative to public schooling. They are, however, against the subsidization with public monies of such a choice. Senator

Moynihan along with co-sponsor Republican Senator Robert Pack-wood of Oregon introduced legislation in the late 1970s to establish tuition tax credits. Strongly challenged by the NEA and the AFT, the bill was threatened by a veto from President Carter and, con-sequently, did not pass.

Another union victory over tuition tax credits was gained, albeit on a local level, in Washington, D.C. in 1980. The AFT, with the dominant local union in that city, mobilized a powerful coalition of civil rights groups, elected officials and parents to soundly defeat a referendum on tuition tax credits for the national city. This victory buttressed AFT President Shanker's contention that the majority of the public did not want tuition tax credits. Citing a Roper Poll in 1978, Shanker claimed that 64 percent of a random sample of 2,007 adults rejected tuition tax credits.[22]

Shanker exerted more leadership on the issue than did the NEA. Indeed, he even chided the NEA leadership for emphasizing a separate Department of Education over the issue of tuition tax credits. In his 1980 and 1984 presidential campaigns, Ronald Rea-gan pledged support for tuition tax credits. However, the budget crisis relegated the pledge to the back burner of domestic politics.

## RACE

Perhaps the sharpest division between the two teacher unions has come over racial attitudes. The AFT has had a long and proud history in the early years of supporting the civil rights struggle, whereas the NEA came to the movement reluctantly. In a twist of irony, however, the NEA has recently become the more politically liberal on civil rights, and the AFT has pursued a more conserva-tive course.

### The AFT on Race

When the AFT was founded in 1915, it welcomed racially inte-grated locals—a policy the NEA was not to adopt for fifty years. The AFT policy was renewed in 1948 and again in 1957 when it expelled some segregated local unions, at a time when member-ship was small. Moreover, the union filed an amicus curiae brief in support of the appeal to desegregate schools in the *Brown v.*

*Topeka, Kansas* case in 1954. A decade later, the AFT lobbied for passage of the 1964 Civil Rights Act. And the next year, Albert Shanker, president of the New York local, was prominent in the march with Dr. Martin Luther King in Selma, Alabama, for voter registration.

The turning point in the union's racial attitude was the confrontation over community control in New York in the late 1960s, and the ascent of Albert Shanker to the AFT presidency. Support of civil rights actions on the part of the AFT weakened considerably after those dates. The union mainly made token support of extensions of the Voting Rights Act and the Civil Rights Acts of the 1980s. The union leadership became a chief antagonist of affirmative action. In the mid-seventies, the AFT was prominent in filing a brief supporting a white engineer, Alan Bakke, in his fight against preferential admissions to medical school; the NEA, however, supported affirmative action programs.

### Community Control

The greatest challenge to the AFT was the confrontation in New York over community control in the late 1960s. Two short years after being elected president of the United Federation of Teachers, AFL-CIO, the New York flagship local, Albert Shanker faced a bid by black parents to share educational power. Black parents sought formal policy roles at a time when the newly recognized local union was gaining influence in the educational affairs of the city. The resulting confrontation fragmented the city in the bitterest racial division in recent history. That conflict was to change the AFT educational reform agenda and make Shanker a national educational figure.

Some educational historians have largely distorted the struggle. Essentially it was a bid by poor black parents to establish formal roles in policymaking through elected school boards in the cities. This practice was common in the more affluent suburbs, but the city educational structure had only appointed boards. The key idea was citizen participation. It attempted to extend the basic democratic concept of political participation to groups that had been bypassed in the society—namely, the poor. In this respect, the community control concept was part and parcel of the movements of

the 1960s. The New Left young radicals had introduced the idea
of participatory democracy with the Port Huron statement of 1962.
A short time later, the War on Poverty was to emphasize maximum feasible participation of the poor in policymaking. And the
advocates of black power would argue that blacks needed to determine policy over the institutions that governed their lives. This
was all of one piece. The aim was to become part of the process
rather than overthrow the system. In that sense, the idea of participation was a reformist rather than radical ethic.

The chief arguments raised against such participation were the
social science studies that indicated that the poor were politically
apathetic. On the other hand, the reformers argued that such studies only measured the status quo, and with the tumultuous change
of participation, new studies would perhaps show otherwise. It was
believed that the poor did not become involved in political processes because they felt their actions did not directly benefit them.
Once the poor saw a chance of substantive benefit, it was argued,
they would participate. Some studies in the late sixties tended to
corroborate that opinion.[23] One critic, however, was to accuse the
social scientist involved with the community control struggle as
"playing a dangerous game by experimenting with his 'theories' at
the expense of the poor."[24]

The community control struggle was a grass roots movement of
black parents in coalition with black and white academics, foundations, educational leaders and the city administration of Mayor John
Lindsay. Some black parents had long been active in the struggle
to integrate New York City schools. When that no longer seemed
possible on a large scale, they turned to community control of the
schools. They contended that their running of the schools could be
no worse than the existing state of massive student failure.

The facts of the dispute were relatively simple. After parents
and black leaders protested in Harlem in 1966, a mini-revolution
quickly spread throughout the city. Mayor Lindsay ordered a blue
panel commission to study the problem and make recommendations for decentralizing the system. The commission was chaired
by McGeorge Bundy, president of the Ford Foundation, and it
issued a book-length study that was authored largely by foundation
staff member Mario Fantini and consultant, Queens College Professor Marilyn Gittell. The report recommended 30 to 60 semi-

autonomous school boards with policy-making powers and with members to be elected only by parents with children in public schools.

During the time of the assembling of the report, a temporary measure was initiated by Mayor Lindsay and the city school board. Three experiments in community control were established: one in Harlem, the original site of the dispute; one in the Ocean Hill–Brownsville section of Brooklyn; and one in the Lower East Side.

The teachers union, under Shanker's leadership, became hostile to the concept of community control. The key issue was over the transfer of thirteen teachers by the Ocean Hill–Brownsville board, a common procedure at the time. The union interpreted the transfers back to central headquarters as a *firing* without due process, and Shanker led a series of city-wide strikes over the issue in the fall of 1968.

Prior to the strikes, the issue of parental involvement through locally elected boards received wide approval in the press, among both education leaders and the general public. The turning point was the raising of the question of black anti-Semitism. Someone distributed a handful of anti-Semitic leaflets in teachers' school mailboxes during the strike in the Ocean Hill–Brownsville district. The union had the few leaflets reproduced into a half million copies and distributed at shopping malls and subway entrances through-out the city.[25] In a city with a large Jewish population (a majority of teachers were Jewish) and significant representation of Jewish citizens in the press and education organizations, black anti-Semi-tism was a grave matter. The result was that "the leaflet united the city's Jewish population behind the AFT," according to David Sel-den, the AFT President.[26] Shanker escalated his rhetoric against the black leaders of the community control movement by describ-ing them as "black gangsters" and "Nazi types."[27] His handling of the strike alarmed even his supporters. A few years later the actor and filmmaker Woody Allen was to insert a bitter remark concern-ing Shanker in his movie *Sleeper*. Awakened in a future world that had undergone a nuclear holocaust, the Woody Allen character was told that the nuclear war was the result of a man named Albert Shanker getting hold of nuclear warheads.

Shanker won the legislative struggle in the state legislature. The political pressure of the union on legislators succeeded in obtaining a diluted decentralization bill that would include all citizens not only parents, to vote on school elections under a complicated proportional representation mechanism. Shanker declared that if the bill sponsored by Mayor Lindsay "passes, I will follow every legislator around who voted for it and kill them [sic] politically."[28] The end result was that school board elections were dominated by organized groups such as representatives of the Catholic Church and the UFT, the latter being a clear conflict of interest.

There were other side effects. The confrontation over community control had made Shanker, in the words of one educator, "a major, if not entirely welcome, force in American education."[29] According to AFT President David Selden, a one-time mentor of Shanker, the confrontation "led to his control of the national union . . . (since) no one else even approached his following among teacher union members."[30]

However, the racial undertones of the strike had negative effects on the prospects for teacher unity. Selden, the chief architect of the unity movement, claimed that the NEA became cool after union merger talks, "citing the union's (UFT) opposition to community control as anti-black."[31] Selden assessed Shanker's actions as being a watershed in the latter's career and that "never again would the former Socialist be able to get back on the high road of progressivism."[32]

In order to repair his image, UFT President Shanker struck on a brilliant stroke that was eventually to help propel him as the main spokesman for teachers during the past two decades. The year after the Ocean Hill–Brownsville confrontation, he persuaded the editors of the *New York Times*, already chagrined by their early editorial support of community control, to publish an educational column by him as a paid advertisement. It was the first time that either the *New York Times* or any other major newspaper did so. Moreover, the *Times* published Shanker's column in the reflective pages of *The Week in Review* Sunday section, the most analytical and thoughtful part of its coverage. The union spends over $100,000 yearly in publishing the Shanker column.[33] It became for over a decade-and-a-half the only major educational commentary and was to be syndicated in other papers. The column was thoughtful, well written and timely, albeit with a special point of view. Rather belatedly, the NEA followed suit some sixteen years later, and NEA

President Mary Hatwood Futrell began writing a paid educational column in the "rival" *Washington Post*. The Futrell column, however, lacked the polemical toughness of the Shanker columns.

Nearly two decades after Ocean Hill, Shanker has been able to refurbish a somewhat tarnished image. As neo-conservative educational historian Diane Ravitch points out, Shanker's new image as an educational statesman has been a "tribute to his staying power."[34] In 1985, the prestigious *Phi Delta Kappan* would select him as one of but four major leaders in education, and describe him as "one of education's and the labor movement's most creative thinkers."[35] The new image was partly the result of the AFT under Shanker having become allied with the "excellence" reform movement, a strategy that elicited from the editors of the *New York Times* the comment that "only recently . . . did (he) also become a consistent advocate of progressive education."[36]

But it was left to Chester E. Finn, Jr., to bestow the ultimate accolade:

For the most part, the direction of change recommended by the excellence movement was compatible with the priorities of the AFT, and support for many of its points could be gleaned from policy resolutions passed at AFT conventions over the years. Albert Shanker is a gifted reader of political entrails, and he concluded far sooner than most other educators that a rare window of opportunity has opened. . . .

The poverty of imagination within the education profession is so severe—at least with regard to issues of quality—that an individual with acuity, energy, and articulateness of Albert Shanker can rapidly emerge as a major statesman, with influence far beyond the ranks of his own organization's membership.[37]

Still, there were critics, for the most part, allied with the "old" equity reform agenda. Former AFT President David Selden, whom Shanker deposed as president in a bitter fight in 1974, considered his former friend as having changed the direction of the AFT for the worse. One scholar would mark Shanker as a "centrist conservative" who was detrimental to the best interests of education.[38]

## The NEA on Race

On the other hand, the NEA was slow to acknowledge the civil rights movement. It took the NEA three years after the *Brown*

decision outlawing school segregation to support it. Moreover, the
NEA did not adopt a resolution outlawing racial discrimination
among its membership until the week that the U.S. Congress passed
the Civil Rights Act of 1964—the height of the civil rights movement. Two years later, the NEA took a step away from segregated
locals by merging with the black American Teachers Association.[39]

The NEA had maintained segregated locals since 1896 and the
Supreme Court decision in *Plessy* v. *Ferguson,* upholding separate
but equal. By the late sixties, NEA locals were integrated.

The NEA had its critics on its handling of civil rights. One scholar
felt that essentially the NEA "reacted to events rather than provided real leadership in the civil rights struggle."[40] Its organizational structure was perceived as preventing black members from
rising to leadership positions. This changed in 1973 when a constitutional revision ensured that NEA leadership councils would
guarantee black representation. Moreover, the NEA was criticized
by black leaders for its silence on the *Brown* school decision outlawing segregation. And between 1955 to 1959, there were no NEA
publications on segregation, at a time when the issue had re-
vived.[41] It was with some irony, these critics felt, that NEA officials could brand Albert Shanker a racist because of his opposition
to community control.

Nevertheless, despite a slow start, the NEA gathered momentum in fighting racism in the 1970s, eventually overshadowing its
rival, the AFT. By the end of the 1970s, some of the NEA leadership was black, and 28 percent of the executive and professional
staff of the NEA were black.[42] NEA publications would offer books
and cassettes on multiethnic education, racism and sexism in schools.
A black teacher, Mary Hatwood Futrell, would be elected president in 1984.

### Affirmative Action

Perhaps the key racial issue dividing the two teacher unions was
affirmative action. The NEA supported the concept, whereas the
AFT opposed it. This difference extended to two cases decided by
the Supreme Court, one in 1976 over admissions to a medical school,
and the other in 1986 involving the layoff of white teachers. In

addition, the NEA had structured a preferential system in its organization to enable blacks to hold office.

Affirmative action called for minorities, especially blacks and women to be given preference when candidates' qualifications were equal for jobs and for admission to schools. Proponents maintained that special consideration was necessary to redress past discrimination. Such a policy, it was argued, was essential to give members of groups that had suffered discrimination an opportunity to catch up in the competitive economic race. On the other hand, opponents presented an equally strong case that such special consideration in effect constituted reverse discrimination, unfairly penalizing qualified white members of the majority society.

The two Supreme Court cases involved the competing teacher unions on opposite sides of the issue. Both cases were lost by the pro-affirmative action groups. However, the decisions were sufficiently ambivalent as to give support, in principle, to the concept of affirmative action.

The first case concerned a preferential admissions system for a medical school. In the mid-1970s, Allan Bakke, a white middle-aged engineer, interested in a career change, contended that he had been unjustly discriminated against by the medical school at the University of California at Davis. Bakke claimed that he was denied admission, despite superior academic credentials, on the basis of a quota system at the school. The Davis program maintained a dual system of admissions, with the majority of places awarded on a traditional basis but sixteen places to be reserved solely to minority applicants. Because of his age, Bakke had been turned down by other medical schools. Nevertheless, the California Supreme Court ruled in his favor, citing his strong academic credentials. The case was appealed to the U.S. Supreme Court.

Both the NEA and the AFT filed briefs as friends of the court that took contrary positions. The NEA strongly urged the Court to rule in the medical school's favor. The NEA presented three main points: (1) affirmative action programs, such as that at Davis, were not unconstitutional; (2) the admission program at Davis met strict standards; and (3) there were no realistic alternatives to such a "race-conscious special admissions policy as a means of including minorities" in medical school.[43] Moreover, the NEA pointed out that a study of minority school graduates indicated that affirmative action programs were effective, since 90 percent of minority students graduated from medical school—a higher succcess rate than that for whites.[44]

The position of the AFT could not be more at variance. In its amicus curiae brief in support of Bakke, the AFT argued two main points: (1) that the Davis formula was "essentially a quota system," which was invalid under the Fourteenth Amendment; and (2) that what was needed were programs open to everyone.[45] The AFT concluded in its brief that it was concerned "whether the public interest is served by remedial educational programs that were founded upon or resulted in preferential benefits to some solely on the basis of race or national orgin."[46]

The *Bakke* case had become a national issue attracting extensive media coverage. The decision by the Supreme Court left both sides claiming victory, while not entirely satisfying either. Four justices ruled in favor of the medical school, and four justices ruled in support of Bakke. The pivotal and deciding vote by Justice Lewis Powell was equally ambivalent. Powell agreed with the first group that race indeed can be a factor in admissions programs, but also agreed with the second group that the specific Davis program was unconstitutional. Therefore, Bakke was to be admitted to the Davis medical school.

Most civil rights spokesmen interpreted the *Bakke* decision as devastating to affirmative action. Others considered positive the Court's emphasis on race being a factor in admissions. They felt that although the Davis program was faulty, other preferential programs might be permissible.

AFT President Shanker considered the *Bakke* decision a "mixed bag." He wondered how the American public would react to the *Bakke* decision, since he felt that the case was based on "real fears" of American citizens. He contended that the American public was concerned that quotas would result in less qualified candidates given preference "on the basis of race." Shanker's alternative to affirmative action was a vague call for more effective schooling for blacks and other minorities:

The key to affirmative action without quotas is education. We should not wait until the applicant is at the door of medical or law school and then decide to overlook educational deficiencies to give special treatment. . . . It is in the elementary and secondary school where we should counteract the effects of poverty and discrimination.[47]

In *Wygant* v. *Jackson Board of Education,* the second affirmative action case decided by the Court in 1986, the case concerned teacher job security. Most important, the local affiliate of the NEA was directly involved. In Jackson, Michigan, the board of education and the NEA affiliate agreed to a layoff plan that would protect recently hired black teachers. This would change the scenario for blacks as being "last hired, first fired." On the other hand, this plan would disregard traditional union seniority provisions. Dismissed white teachers sued. The lower courts found the Jackson plan acceptable, and the plaintiffs appealed to the Supreme Court.

The Supreme Court ruled in favor of the dismissed teachers, 5 to 4. Again the results were mixed. Although the Court found that the Jackson plan was too hard on innocent parties and was not designed narrowly enough, the justices upheld the concept of affirmative action. Justice Lewis Powell expressed the feelings of a majority of the Court when he declared that "in order to remedy the effect of past discrimination, it may be necessary to take race into account."[48]

In July 1986, the Supreme Court further clarified its position on affirmative action, ruling in the affirmative. In two separate cases, one involving fire fighters in Cleveland and one involving sheet metal–workers in New York City, the Court determined that the preferential hiring and promotion programs in those cities were appropriate. In the Cleveland case, the Court voted, 6 to 3, in the affirmative to support affirmative action. In the New York case, the Court voted more closely, by a 5 to 4 margin, but went a step further by endorsing a specific percentage of 29 percent for the minority membership goal of the sheet metal–union. The Reagan administration regarded the decisions as "disappointing" and "extremely unfortunate."[49] But the decisions clarified a rather ambivalent and ambiguous position of the Supreme Court in favor of affirmative action.

There were other signs of disagreement over race between the two teacher unions. Most important, the NEA in the early seventies had restructured its organization so that minorities could be elected to leadership positions. The AFT condemned the practice as using quotas, which it abhorred.

At issue was a crucial difference in assumptions concerning race. The NEA leadership acted from the belief that racial discrimination still existed substantively, whereas the AFT held that racism had been sufficiently checked and that affirmative action was tilting the balance the other way. In this respect, the leadership of the two organizations reflected wider views in the society. Most blacks, along with some white allies, considered racism to be as strong as ever, despite some economic and social gains made by the civil rights revolution. Conservatives on the other hand, had felt, for the most part, that racial discrimination was a matter of the past.

This view could best be illustrated by a debate between the two teacher unions over a publication of the NEA. The NEA had published a booklet on the Ku Klux Klan entitled "Violence, The Ku Klux Klan and the Struggle for Equality." In that instructional manual, the NEA asserted that the Klan "feeds on a climate of general social acceptance of racism; and that a variety of social and economic indicators demonstrate that the gap between whites and blacks had widened, not lessened."[50]

AFT President Shanker took offense. He retorted that blacks had made significant progress. He lambasted the NEA for its "false and harmful" booklet, which taught that "our society is innately racist."[51] This again was an example, Shanker claimed, of the NEA using the public schools "to propagandize for one particular ideology."[52]

This disparity on racial views damaged the prospects for teacher unity. Race was considered as one of four major obstacles to be resolved between the two organizations during merger talks.[53] Both the NEA and the AFT claimed the other maintained a racist philosophy. The AFT wanted the NEA to relinquish its guarantees for black representation in its leadership, which the NEA steadfastly refused.


**FOREIGN POLICY**

Perhaps the most removed ideological difference between the two teacher unions has been their sporadic views on foreign policy.

This is the least important, in the sense, that the issue affects teachers only indirectly. Nevertheless, the two unions have disagreed sharply over the conduct of foreign policy by the United States. Under Shanker (but not under Selden), the AFT generally supported the AFL-CIO position of a strong military defense and a vigorous anti-communism. On the other hand, the NEA, under Herndon and his successor, Don Cameron, has pursued a general disarmament and pro-peace movement stance.

It must be pointed out that the two organizations on this and many issues are strongly influenced by its top leadership. One example had been when Selden, past president of the AFT, had led the union to support Senator George McGovern for the presidency in 1972—the first support for a presidential candidate by a teacher union. Under Selden's leadership, the AFT had also been critical of the Vietnam War. Both positions had clearly been counter to AFL-CIO policy.

The shift back to AFL-CIO positions on foreign policy had come with the ascendency of Albert Shanker as president. Shanker was made a vice-president of the AFL-CIO, *before* becoming AFT president, and has become a molder of AFL-CIO policy. Since becoming AFT president, Shanker has steered the AFT into a strong anti-communist camp. Shanker has been a consistent critic of human rights violations in Communist nations, especially the Soviet Union. He has denounced Soviet anti-Semitism and acclaimed such anti-communist movements as the Solidarity labor movement in Poland. On balance, however, he has not criticized human rights violations and repression by U.S. allies, especially in Latin America. Concomitantly, the NEA, while criticizing United States foreign policy, has not been a regular critic of Soviet actions.

The NEA, under Executive Director Terry Herndon in the 1970s to early 1980s, has projected an image that its critics label as New Left radicalism. Certainly, Herndon was greatly concerned with the issue of peace. It became a near obsession with the former teacher. His book of speeches, *We, The Teachers*, contains a large section of addresses on the subject of peace. Herndon linked peace with the very essence of the teaching profession—a rather daring if somewhat nebulous move. He says:

I see more clearly now than I ever have that it is not possible for us to do the job for education while ignoring the economic and policy environment in which we try to do that job. If we do not deal with quetions such as . . . the creeping militarism that is enveloping the capacity of this country to serve and care about people, we will lose the fight for education and the fight for decency.[54]

Anybody who cares about education but wanders through Washington oblivious to economic and military policy is doing nothing productive.[55]

Herndon coupled his passion for peace with angry words for President Reagan. He termed Reagan's first budget, with its increased military spending, "a moral outrage."[56] He compared the Reagan foreign policy to George Orwell's *1984*.

Even more outrageous, it commits a peace-loving people to the acceleration of a bizarre adventure in militarism as the means of national security. We are told in 1984, like the followers of Orwell's Big Brother, we will accept the delusion that "War is Peace." It will not be so for me.[57]

Herndon and the NEA leadership's sentiments were part of an international peace movement that grew in intensity. Limited to the United States and Western democratic nations, this peace movement has focused attention on nuclear war and disarmament. In the United States, the peace movement had been dubbed "the freeze" movement, that is, the attempt to freeze arms escalation at current levels. This "freeze movement" consists of a broad coalition of clergy, scientists, physicians, academics and national political leaders such as Senator Ted Kennedy, as well as ordinary citizens. Nevertheless, President Reagan enjoyed enormous popularity, and the invasions of Grenada and the bombing of Libya were widely supported by the public.

The leadership of the churches have been outspoken in opposition to the arms race. In 1983, the American bishops of the Roman Catholic Church strongly denounced nuclear war in a pastoral letter, *The Challenge of Peace*. However, the bishops equivocated on the equally important concept of deterrence, refraining from "saying a definitive 'no' to deterrence."[58] Three years afterward, the Bishops of the United Methodist Church issued their pastoral letter that went one step further than the Catholics. In their pastoral letter, *In Defense of Creation: The Nuclear Crisis and a Just Peace*, the Methodists rejected the concept of nuclear deterrence. This position was based on a "lack of confidence in proposed 'defenses' against nuclear attack."[59] Moreover, the Methodist bishops believed that the military costs of an arms build-up were "prohibitive" and a "social justice issue" since it was felt that military spending would displace domestic social spending.[60] The Reagan policy was that nuclear war was permissible, on a limited basis, and that the United States would not renounce the option to strike first as had been done by the Soviet Union.

The freeze movement included such groups as the Union for Concerned Scientists, the Federation of American Scientists and Physicians for Social Responsibility, in addition to the church groups. In 1982 the Union for Concerned Scientists convened a convocation on nuclear war on 151 campuses. By Spring 1983, nearly three-quarters of a million citizens marched in a nuclear war protest in New York City. Similar demonstrations were held in Europe. However, only a handful of colleges and universities, estimated at slightly over twenty, inaugurated peace studies programs, although most of those schools were elite universities such as Princeton and Stanford.[61] Still, the peace movement could be said to represent a minority view in the United States.

The NEA officially went on record opposing nuclear conflict. In its 1981 meeting of the Representative Assembly, the 9,000 delegates resolved the following:

The Association urges that the nations of the world, through cooperative talks, develop treaties and disarmament agreements that reduce the danger of nuclear wars and free resources for important domestic problems.[62]

But the incident that stirred the most controversy was the publication by the NEA of a teacher's manual on nuclear war. In March 1983, the NEA published the manual *Choices: A Unit on Conflict and Nuclear War*. The teaching unit drew criticism from President Reagan and AFT President Shanker, among others.

The NEA teaching manual was written by the Union of Concerned Scientists, a pro-freeze organization, in collaboration with the Massachusetts Teachers Association. Some of the books referred to in the bibliography of the teaching unit include pro-freeze treatises by such advocates as Senators Ted Kennedy and Mark Hatfield.[63]

Harvard psychiatrist John E. Mack attempted to explain the rationale of the teaching manual in a foreword. He explained that school children have developed fears over the prospect of nuclear war and that a teaching manual was necessary to inform students of facts and possible alternatives. He cited studies that indicated that the nuclear arms race has had "a significantly adverse impact on the emotional lives of young people in the United States and other countries."[64]

The unit hoped to raise "fundamental questions about conflict, war, and nuclear weapons . . . (and) it is designed to highlight both historical decisions on nuclear weapons and the choices available when considering the future roles of these weapons."[65] The lessons were structured so that a teacher could cover the material in a minimum of ten class periods over a period of two to four weeks. Nine lessons include material on the adverse effects of nuclear war, the escalation of the arms race, student perceptions concerning U.S.–Soviet relations and alternatives to nuclear conflict. The unit was field-tested in thirty-four states. However, by April 1986 only 15,000 of these teaching manuals had been sold—a rather miniscule figure compared to the 1.8 million membership of the NEA.[66]

The manual attempts to discuss the volatile subject of nuclear war from a balanced perspective, with varying results. For example, in the account of the bombing of Hiroshima, both sides of the argument are presented. On the one hand, the case is made that President Harry Truman's decision to drop atomic bombs on Japan might have shortened the war. On the other hand, the argument is presented that the act was "overkill," and that a simple demonstration of the awesome effects of the atomic bomb might have brought the same results without damaging a civilian population.

The material is presented with a strong accent on prevention. The authors have raised the alarming speculation that within a decade as many as twenty-six nations—some of them with unstable politics—will develop nuclear arsenals. The clear implication is that the overriding concern is for a nuclear freeze and a check on any use of nuclear weapons.

AFT President Albert Shanker branded the teaching unit "pro-

paganda." He accused the NEA of attempting to have teachers
"press one viewpoint."[67] The NEA, he charged, should not bring
"political, moral and economic issues" into the classroom.[68] NEA's
Terry Herndon replied that "teaching is emphatically moral and
beset by extraordinary moral responsibility."[69]

Shanker was worried over the condemnation of an escalating arms
race. He challenged the lesson plan as alarmist, "loaded with moving accounts by the survivors of Hiroshima and Nagasaki." Moreover, he scored the manual for its silence on the strong military
position of the Soviet Union, implying that the United States needed
to achieve parity. For Shanker the unit is not sufficiently anti-So-
viet and anti-communist:

There is no discussion of the Soviet takeover of other countries, no treatment of Soviet aid to Communists around the world to help overthrow
other governments . . . no facts on the Soviet political system . . . the
Gulags, the psychiatric tortures. . . . The NEA action will further undermine public confidence in public education—and it has seriously damaged
the NEA's ability to prevent schools from being used for indoctrination by
other groups.[70]

NEA officials replied that they "suspected (Shanker) of brushing
his teeth with gunpowder."[71]

The reaction within the field of education to the teacher's manual was predictable. On the one hand, political conservatives such
as Chester E. Finn, Jr., would criticize the NEA for its "generally
uncritical stance toward Moscow."[72] He would praise the AFT for
its "general position on national defense (as being) consistent with
the AFL-CIO's view that strength begets security."[73] And the reaction by the Reagan administration on peace studies was loudly
antagonistic. Secretary of Education William Bennett would characterize the peace studies movement as a "threat . . . from the
left and lost . . . in shorthand, Marx and Marx Brothers."[74] On
the other hand, moderates such as Stanley E. Elam, former longtime editor of *Phi Delta Kappan*, would praise the NEA as the
"organizational leader in action oriented (peace) programs from school
implementation."[75]

Another dispute between the NEA and the AFT on foreign policy had occurred earlier in 1978. In that case the NEA had lent its

name and considerable prestige as a sponsor to a documentary on the Soviet Union during the Second World War that drew controversy. Allegations were made that the program was too sympathetic to the Soviets, and that, in fact, it only told their side of the story. However, the documentary, entitled "The Unknown War," was shown on public television. It had seemingly establishment credentials. The series was underwritten by Hanover Trust and the Eaton Corporation. It was written by a popular commercial poet, Rod McKuen, and narrated by the respected actor Burt Lancaster.

AFT President Shanker, along with officials from such anti-communist agencies as Freedom House, objected to the thrust of the documentary series. According to Shanker, not only did the series neglect to mention the human rights abuses of Stalin in the 1930s, but final script approval lay with the Soviets. Shanker charged that "the series should be greeted with as much indignation as would greet a similar cover-up of Nazi enemies or the history of American slavery."[76]

In summary, the ideological differences between the two teacher unions have been considerable. The aims of the unions in education, on matters of race and social policy and on foreign policy were pursued in the political arena, sometimes with great controversy. One could characterize the NEA as having been to the political left of center for the past two decades, whereas the AFT has moved from the political left to right of center.

## NOTES

1. Albert Shanker, "No Reason for Separate Education Department," *New York Times*, March 4, 1979, p. E7.

2. Albert Shanker, "Sometimes the Administration Is Right," *New York Times*, October 13, 1985, p. E7.

3. Harold O. Johns, "The National Teachers Examination—A Closer Look" (Norfolk, Va., 1986), p. 2.

4. David R. Krathwohl, "The National Teacher Examination and Professional Standards," *Education Leadership*, February 1983, p. 75.

5. Walter Mercer, "The Gathering Storm: Teacher Testing and Black Teachers," *Education Leadership*, February 1983, p. 70.

6. Albert Shanker, "Will Testing Knock Out Minorities?" *New York Times*, May 19, 1985, p. E7.

7. Johns, "The National Teachers Examination—A Closer Look," p. 14.

8. Albert Shanker, "When Testing Teachers May Be Hoax," *New York Times*, July 21, 1985, p. E9.

9. *New York Times*, May 9, 1986, p. A16.

10. *New York Times*, May 16, 1986, p. A17.

11. Ibid.

12. Mary Hatwood Futrell, "New Report, Old Truths," *Education Week*, May 28, 1986, p. 20.

13. Maurice R. Berube, "The Trouble with Vouchers," *Commonweal*, January 29, 1971, p. 415.

14. David K. Cohen and Eleanor Farrar, "Power to the Parents: The Story of Education Vouchers," *Public Interest*, Summer 1977.

15. Berube, "The Trouble with Vouchers," p. 415.

16. Ibid.

17. Ibid.

18. Albert Shanker, "Holland's Public Education Vanishing," *New York Times*, July 4, 1982, p. E9.

19. Albert Shanker, "Voucher Proposal: Nose of the Camel," *New York Times*, November 17, 1985, p. E7.

20. Mary Hatwood Futrell, "Vouchers: The Hoax Is Transparent," *Washington Post*, December 15, 1985, p. C3.

21. Heidi Steffer, "Vouchers: Chance, Not Choice," *NEA Today*, December 19, 1985, p. 6.

22. Albert Shanker, "64% Reject Private School Tuition Aid," *New York Times*, August 6, 1978, p. E7.

23. For example, Marilyn Gittell, with Maurice R. Berube et al., *Local Control in Education* (New York: Praeger, 1972).

24. Chaim I. Waxman, *The Stigma of Poverty* (New York: Pergamon Press, 1983), p. 110.

25. David Selden, *The Teacher Rebellion* (Washington, D.C.: Howard University Press, 1985) p. 153.

26. Ibid.

27. Maurice R. Berube and Marilyn Gittell, eds., *Confrontation at Ocean Hill–Brownsville* (New York: Praeger, 1969), p. 147.

28. Sol Stern, " 'Scab' Teachers," in Berube and Gittell, *Confrontation at Ocean Hill–Brownsville*, p. 185.

29. George R. Kaplan, "Shining Lights in High Places: Education's Top Four Leaders and Their Heirs," *Phi Delta Kappan*, September 1985, p. 12.

30. Selden, *The Teacher Rebellion*, p. 155.

31. Ibid., p. 156.

32. Ibid.

33. Kaplan, "Education's Top Four Leaders and Their Heirs," p. 12.

34. Diane Ravitch, *The Troubled Crusade: American Education 1945–1980* (New York: Basic Books, 1983), p. 315.

35. Kaplan, "Education's Top Four Leaders and Their Heirs," p. 13.

36. *New York Times*, January 2, 1986, p. A18.

37. Chester E. Finn, Jr., "Teacher Unions and School Quality: Potential Allies or Inevitable Foes?" *Phi Delta Kappan*, January 1985, p. 334.

38. Fred L. Pincus, "From Equity to Excellence: The Rebirth of Educational Conservatism," in Beatrice Gross and Ronald Gross, *The Great School Debate* (New York: Simon and Schuster, 1985), p. 338.

39. Allan M. West, *The National Education Association: The Power Base for Education* (New York: Free Press, 1980), p. 103.

40. Rolland Dewing, "The NEA and Minority Rights," *The Journal of Negro Education*, 47 (Fall 1978), p. 379.

41. Ibid., p. 382.

42. West, *The National Education Association: The Power Base for Education*, p. 105.

43. National Education Association, "Bakke: Pro and Con," *Phi Delta Kappan*, March 1978, p. 450.

44. Ibid., p. 447.

45. American Federation of Teachers, AFL-CIO, "Bakke: Pro and Con," *Phi Delta Kappan*, March 1978, p. 451.

46. Ibid., p. 455.

47. Albert Shanker, "High Court *Bakke* Ruling: A Mixed Bag," *New York Times*, July 9, 1978, p. E7.

48. *New York Times*, May 24, 1986, p. 22.

49. *New York Times*, July 3, 1986, p. B9.

50. Albert Shanker, "How Not to Teach About the KKK," *New York Times*, November 1, 1981, p. E9.

51. Ibid.

52. Ibid.

53. Kenneth P. Lubetsky, "Will the NEA and the AFT Ever Merge?" *The Educational Forum*, 41 (March 1977), p. 312.

54. Terry Herndon, *We, The Teachers: Terry Herndon on Education and Democracy* (Cabin John, Md.: Seven Locks Press, 1983), p. 117.

55. Ibid., p. 134.

56. Ibid., p. 122.

57. Ibid.

58. Editors, "Time to Accept the Challenge," *Commonweal*, May 6, 1983, p. 260.

59. *New York Times*, April 27, 1986, p. A34.

60. Ibid.

61. Stanley E. Elam, "Educators and the Nuclear Threat," *Phi Delta Kappan*, April 1983, pp. 533-34.

62. Terry Herndon, "A Teacher Speaks of Peace," *Phi Delta Kappan*, April 1983, p. 530.

63. Union of Concerned Scientists, *Choices: A Unit on Conflict and Nuclear War* (Washington, D.C.: National Education Association, 1983), p. 94.

64. Ibid., p. 4.

65. Ibid.

66. Telephone Interview with Dave Powell, NEA Publications Officer, April 24, 1986.

67. Albert Shanker, "NEA Trying to Teach—or Indoctrinate?" *New York Times*, April 17, 1983, p. E7.

68. Ibid.

69. Herndon, "A Teacher Speaks of Peace," p. 531.

70. Shanker, "NEA Trying to Teach—or Indroctrinate?" p. E7.

71. Chester E. Finn, Jr., "Teacher Politics," *Commentary*, February 1983, p. 37.

72. Ibid., p. 39.

73. Ibid., p. 37.

74. *Virginia Ledger-Star*, April 11, 1986, p. A10.

75. Elam, "Educators and the Nuclear Threat," p. 537.

76. Albert Shanker, "NEA Endorses Soviet Propaganda," *New York Times*, December 10, 1978, p. E9.

# 6

# The Challenge of School Reform

The school reform movement of the 1980s redirected the goals and process of schooling in America. This reform movement, aptly dubbed the "excellence" movement, was created by the influence of a number of concomitant educational studies, commissioned and written independently of one another, that proposed essentially similar ojectives. That message was that American students compared unfavorably with foreign counterparts and, therefore, education must be strengthened. For the most part, the excellence movement placed the two teacher unions, in varying measure, on the defensive.

The National Education Association was suspicious of school reform. NEA officials interpreted criticism of the schools as attacks on teachers. Moreover, the NEA was committed more to educating the disadvantaged rather than the "best and brightest." By contrast, the American Federation of Teachers became more comfortable with the "excellence" reform movement. AFT President Albert Shanker perceived school reform to be the entrée for professional control of teaching. But the bottom line was that school reform once more, emerged from *outside* the confines of the educational establishment. The teacher unions were mainly reactors to public pressures.

## SCHOOL REFORM

The excellence movement has three major impacts. First, the studies generated widespread interest in education once again, so that education became a national issue for the first time since the 1960s. Second, the substance of these studies was to shift the emphasis on education from that of helping the disadvantaged—which had been the focus of educational policy since the Great Society of the sixties—to that of preparing the best and brightest to compete in an increasingly technological, global society. Finally, the excellence movement occasioned a transfer of educational influence to the states from the federal government, where the accent had been since the launching of Sputnik in the 1950s.

Most important, the excellence movement put the teacher unions in a position of reacting to initiatives from government. The larger NEA viewed the recommendations of the excellence reports with caution and skepticism, whereas AFT's Shanker became almost single-handedly a teacher spokesman for raising educational standards. Ironically, the excellence movement enlisted a strange constituency of mostly political leaders—painfully aware of strong economic competition from abroad without strong support from the natural educational constituency of parents, teachers and students.

The school reform movement can be said to have been born in April 1983. It was then that the key document, A Nation at Risk: The Imperative for School Reform, was published. This document was the work of the National Commission on Excellence in Education, a task force that had been created by the Secretary of Education Terence Bell two years earlier. The commission dramatized what it considered the deteriorating quality of American education and the urgent need for school reform. "If an unfriendly foreign power had attempted to impose on America the mediocre educational performance that exists today," the authors dramatically proclaimed, "we might have well viewed it as an act of war."[1] The commission report was supplemented by a plethora of studies and analyses but of varying quality, with similar conclusions.

These studies included John Goodlad's study of schooling, Ernest Boyer and his study of American high schools, Mortimer Adler's Paideia Proposal, a study by the Task Force on Economic Growth, one from the Business-Higher Education Forum, and others. The essence of the message was, for the most part, the same: American schools were failing in the race to develop brain power for a highly sophisticated technocracy. And the solutions proposed struck a similar chord: raise standards, strengthen curriculum, and improve the quality of teachers.

The excellence movement did not materialize from nowhere. As has been the case with all great school reform movements in our history, the impetus for reform came from societal forces outside education. Just as the political reforms of progressivism encouraged the progressive school movement, and Sputnik launched science reforms and the civil rights movement focused on the need to improve education for the disadvantaged, the excellence movement also was occasioned by other than purely educational concerns. It was a response to the emerging technological superiority of competing friendly democratic societies, especially Japan. Japanese technological success had an adverse impact on the American economy. The most glaring disparity was the fact that the Japanese produced better cars than we did in Detroit. This success was replicated in other industries by other friendly nations in the free world. The authors of *A Nation at Risk* made a point of referring to this declining state of American industrial strength. This decline had resulted in the short run in a cottage industry for publishing houses with books on American and Japanese management techniques to improve product and productivity, and regain a competitive edge. Understandably, it was only a matter of time before the scrutiny placed on business leadership would be transferred to education.

The excellence movement had numerous, vocal supporters. Ernest Boyer, president of the Carnegie Foundation, would hail the reform movement as "the best opportunity we will have during this century to improve American education."[2] Perhaps the most ardent champion of reform, Chester E. Finn, Jr., assistant secretary of education, would proclaim the reform movement "of epochal proportions."[3]

However, the excellence movement was not without critics. Professor Michael Kirst of the University of California, would pessimistically chide that the excellence reform movement "will probably last no more than three years."[4] More damaging, Colin Greer and Marilyn Gittell, professors of education and political science respectively, would condemn the movement as a "new elitism"

that does not "place democratic values in the forefront."[5] But it
was left, however, to David Selden, former president of the AFT,
to perceive the movement as a "direct attack on the public schools
and teachers."[6]

## THREE MAJOR IMPACTS OF THE EXCELLENCE
## REPORTS

The excellence studies made education a national issue once again.
The media discovered a viable subject and from television to academic journals the meaning and influence of the national studies
were scrutinized, in particular, A Nation at Risk. One survey showed
that over 700 articles in major newspapers had dealt with education reform four months after the publication of A Nation at Risk.[7]
No less than a dozen major telecasts on the state of education were
broadcast on major networks a year after the government report.[8]
Over two dozen articles on school reform were published in the
academic journal of the education profession, Phi Delta Kappan,
in twenty-five issues over a two-and-a-half year period following
the federal reports. In addition, the large majority of these articles
were supportive of the excellence reform thrust. Most important,
polls showed that in the 1984 presidential campaign, the American
public considered education to be second in importance only to
unemployment as a campaign issue—higher than foreign policy or
the pressing issue of the federal deficit.[9] For the first time since
the 1960s education became a national concern.

There was a special irony to this newfound interest in education.
Conservatives had held that public schooling was not a national
issue. In 1980, Ronald Reagan had campaigned on the pledge to
eliminate the Department of Education, created by President Jimmy
Carter at the urging of the NEA. Reagan's first Secretary of Education, Terence Bell, looked forward to the day when such an
eventuality might take place. One indication of the low priority
conservatives placed on public education as a national issue was
exemplified by Chester E. Finn's analysis in his book on the role
of Richard Nixon in education, Education and the Presidency. Finn
declared that education held extremely low priority on the presidential agenda because of its "lowly status," caused in large part
by the small role the federal government could play constitution-

ally.[10] President Reagan pragmatically reversed his stand on the Department of Education after witnessing the fallout generated by the department's *A Nation at Risk*, and made education a campaign issue in 1984.

The second major impact of the excellence reports was that they caused a substantive shift in educational direction. For nearly a generation, policymakers in Washington and on state and local levels had concentrated on the disadvantaged—the lower socioeconomic groups, comprised of blacks, and other minorities—to the exclusion of other segments of the educational society. This was the thrust of the Great Society programs and the War on Poverty, which had been substantially maintained through the 1970s. Emphasis was on compensatory education and programs such as Head Start that would help the children of the poor. To a large extent, the concern, as well as program monies, was more for the disadvantaged rather than the gifted.

On the other hand, the essence of the excellence movement was to strengthen programs for the best and the brightest who could successfully compete in an increasingly technological society. Some of the "old" reformers of the 1960s, such as former Commissioner of Education (in the Johnson administration) Harold Howe II, perceived this subtle shift and worried about it. Howe was concerned, for example, about the "unfinished equity agenda."[11] Indeed, some of these "old" reformers pointed out that this shift in educational emphasis came at a time when some progress was being made in educating the poor. Such Great Society innovations as Title I programs for the poor and Head Start pre-schooling were now achieving educational payoffs. Title I programs were beginning to reveal significant incremental educational gains in most major cities by the late 1970s.[12] Longitudinal studies of Head Start, done over a twenty-year period, showed dramatic long-range gains both academically and socially.[13] Moreover, the research of such "effective school" scholars as Michael Rutter and Wilbur Brookover indicated that certain school strategies appeared to be successful with low-income students.[14]

The emergence of the excellence reform movement raised the question of whether America can have an emphasis on *both* excellence and equity. Some educational historians point out that in the twentieth century, American policymakers have pursued either one or the other, suggesting a possible conflict. These historians conclude that in the 1980s the swing to excellence has been the result of the belief of a majority of the American public "that the efforts to create a more equalitarian educational system were made at the expense of quality."[15] However, they conclude that despite such cyclic periods, democracy "requires twin goals for education from which there can be no retreat."[16]

Lastly, the excellence movement spurred a transfer of educational influence and power back to the states. This was also due, in large part, to the conservative philosophy of the Reagan "revolution," which emphasized the importance of the states in domestic issues and the need to decrease the role of the federal government. Whereas the Great Society years launched an unbridled leadership role for the federal government in education, President Reagan and his aides held that the contrary was beneficial. Both Lyndon Johnson and Hubert Humphrey, a former schoolteacher and college professor respectively, believed in a central role for education at the national level. Consequently, educational programs were the cornerstone of the Great Society and the War on Poverty, and more educational legislation was passed during those years than had been enacted in all the past years of the republic, including a historic first aid to education bill.

On the other hand, one of the key tenets of conservative philosophy is that competition is essential to the workings of the economy and the democratic political system. This would mean decreasing the influence of the public sector and increasing that of the private sector. This tenet applies to education as well. Understandably, therefore, the Reagan administration introduced the concept of vouchers in 1986 to enable poor parents given federal monies to choose either competing private or parochial schools rather than public schools.

*A Nation at Risk* clearly spells out the limited role of the federal government as merely having "the *primary responsibility* to identify the national interest in education."[17] The rest was up to the states. In truth, the authors of the report were on sound constitutional grounds. The framers of the Constitution had failed to perceive any importance for education and had neglected to mention it thereby giving states the authority by default. However, education had increased in importance since the Industrial Revolution, and a number of presidents had strengthened the federal hand in education through the back door on a categorical basis, as the occasion required it. One such example was the passing of the National Defense Education Act in 1959 after the trauma of Sputnik in order to strengthen science in the classroom. Federal influence had grown to great proportions, even though the federal dollar share of education nationally was still under 10 percent.

The states moved quickly to assume major responsibility and expand their roles. By 1985, more than thirty-five states had tightened high school graduation requirements.[18] Twenty-one states revised curricula and textbooks, and approximately 290 state commissions were created to scrutinize public education.[19] Policy analysts from the conservative "think tank," the Heritage Foundation, would welcome such "a dizzying number of efforts to improve the schools."[20] They declared that "the leadership that is making it possible (for reform) has come from outside the education community, mostly from the state governments."[21]

Certainly, the excellence reform movement comprised an odd constituency. For the most part, these new reformers were political policymakers rather than the natural constituency of teachers, administrators, parents or average citizens. Although Chester E. Finn, Jr., believed that this was a "very nearly populist movement, led primarily by self-interested parents and employers and by elected officials," the opposite seemed true.[22] Only the latter exerted intense interest in school reform, motivated mostly by the specter of foreign economic competition. This is an issue that has a greater impact on legislators than on the ordinary parent with children in the school, or the teacher teaching those children.

State efforts can be grouped under three main categories: raising academic standards for students, improving the quality of teachers and revising curricula. By 1985, forty-one states, with six deliberating policy, increased high school graduation requirements.[23] In like fashion, thirty-five states, with fourteen pending, had raised teacher preparation and certification requirements in that time.[24] Moreover, four states had devised some kind of merit pay–system or career ladder–program for teachers.[25]

The transfer of educational leadership to the states could not immediately be perceived as good or bad. Although the Heritage Foundation analysts believed that this transfer of power would mean "that the problems and opportunities before us will be confronted differently," it was not clear how the educational policy outcomes—the raising of student achievement and improvement of the condition of education—would be affected.[26] Indeed, these analysts would temper their enthusiasm with a cautionary note that "the jury is out on the states' reform efforts and will be for several years."[27]

Let us examine the thrust of the key excellence study, *A Nation at Risk*, and its educational impact and the response of the two teacher unions. We shall scrutinize the study and its data base and consider the criticisms of it. Then we will analyze the differing responses of both the NEA and the AFT leadership. Finally we will assess the outcomes of the excellence reform movement.

## WHAT *A NATION AT RISK* SAID

The crucial document of the excellence reform movement is *A Nation at Risk*. Commissioned by Secretary of Education Bell in 1981, it was released to the public two years later. It was the work of a specially appointed task force, the National Commission on Excellence in Education, chaired by David P. Gardner, president of the University of Utah. The commission comprised some seventeen members of the educational establishment, only one of whom was a teacher. Five members were from public schools, three were college presidents, one of whom was the president of Yale, and others represented the business world. The commission invited selected scholarly papers from experts and held a limited series of eight hearings. The commission's charge was to "report on the quality of education in America," which, according to Secretary Bell, was cause for concern because of a "widespread public perception that something is seriously remiss in our educational system."[28]

What did the report conclude? In sixty-five pages, the commission authors found that "the educational foundations of our society are presently eroded by a rising tide of mediocrity."[29] Indeed, education was adrift since Americans had "lost sight of the basic purposes of schooling."[30] The commission attempted to accomplish a twofold task: assess the quality of education, focusing mainly on high schools, and compare American student performance with foreign counterparts. Lurking in the background was the fear that

American industry could not recoup past advantages to other sophisticated technological societies. The report's author spoke of the "risk" that America was fast becoming a second-class industrial power.

The risk is not only that the Japanese make automobiles more efficiently than Americans and have government subsidies for development and export. It is not just that the South Koreans recently built the world's most efficient steel mill, or that American machine tools, once the pride of the world, are being replaced by German products. It is also that these developments signify a redistribution of trained capability throughout the globe.[31]

Critics of A *Nation at Risk* scorned the alarmist rhetoric of the report, its inappropriate use of comparative statistics and its misplacing of the blame for the nation's economic slide from business to the schools. They contended that, perhaps, poor management decisions predicated on short-term profits rather than long-term investment, coupled with unfavorable support from government, proved more damaging to America's economic position.

The report cited thirteen academic indicators of academic deterioration in the public schools. Of these, five are major and deserve consideration:

1. Comparisons with advanced, "friendly" countries showed that on nineteen academic tests American students were behind, scoring last seven times.

2. There had been a severe decline in student performance on the Scholastic Aptitude Tests from 1963 to 1980.

3. Many seventeen-year-old youngsters did not register strong abstract intellectual and inferential skills.

4. The same seventeen-year-olds declined in science achievement in 1969, 1973 and 1977.

5. There was a growing tide of illiteracy in the nation.

Of these five major findings by the commission, the first three were severely challenged as to accuracy and reliability, thereby raising questions as to how excellent were the excellence studies. The latter two charges concerning poor achievement on science

criteria and the awareness of significant illiteracy in the nation appeared warranted. Academic critics claimed that the data used in
*A Nation at Risk* was dated, misinterpreted and alarmist in view
of the conclusions reached by the National Commission on Excellence.

The stongest challenge was directed at the accuracy of the statistics on comparative achievement. Lawrence Steadman and Marshall Smith pointed out that the comparative data was dated, having been gathered over a decade from 1964-1971 by the International
Association for the Evaluation of Educational Achievement
(IAEDA).[32] Most important, there was serious question as to the
appropriateness of comparing an open educational system (that of
the United States) with foreign educational systems that were selective. In most nations, socialistic and capitalistic, students proceed to academic high schools and higher education on the basis
of highly selective and competitive academic performance measured by national tests. That is not the case in the United States,
where students proceed to high levels of schooling on less stringent qualifications. Consequently, on a percentage basis, the United
States has more students in high school (75 percent), as well as
college (50 percent), as well as more sheer numbers than any nation in the world. Indeed, Professor Torsten Husen, who founded
the IAEDA and comparative studies, labeled *A Nation at Risk* "an
exercise in comparing the incomparable."[33] For example, only 9
percent of West German youths graduate from high schools, which
are university oriented. When the top 9 percent of American high
school students are compared with international counterparts, such
as the West Germans, they "do better than those in foreign countries at the same level"[34]

The problem with such comparative evaluations is not only with
the appropriateness of the comparison but with basic educational
philosophy as well. The question is one of competing educational
ideologies: one based on meritocracy seeking to promote an elite,
and another based on an open educational system that is geared
more to the social mobility of the many. Moreover, American education appears to be historically unclear in its goals, on the one
hand, seeking excellence, and on the other, equality of opportunity. *A Nation at Risk* fuels the ideological confusion even more.

The authors of that report admit of a possible contradiction in American educational aims:

We do not believe that a public commitment to excellence and educational reform must be made at the expense of a strong public commitment to the equitable treatment of our diverse population. The twin goals of equity and high quality schooling have a profound and practical meaning for our economy and society and we cannot permit one to yield to the other either in principle or in practice.[35]

Others were not so sure that such a fragile relationship could be maintained. Professor Torsten Husen, a key figure in international educational comparisons, offered a simple and blunt solution to the alleged crisis in American education as described by *A Nation at Risk*: Make the American system selective like its European counterparts.[36]

The report's second major charge was that Scholastic Aptitude Test (SAT) scores of students declined from 1963 to 1980. This assertion is equally specious. Although the fact of the matter is that there occurred a drastic decline in test scores of students during that period that only began to stabilize in 1980, that data has been seriously misinterpreted by the authors of *A Nation at Risk*. For one thing, that precipitous decline coincides with a period of tremendous increase of students taking the SAT and going to college. The civil rights movement during that time, for example, had the dual effect of both raising expectations of minority youngsters and opening educational opportunities. Consequently, more students from lower socioeconomic backgrounds, many with poor academic preparation, took the SAT and applied for college. A major study conducted by the College Board found that two-thirds to three-fourths of the decline in SAT scores from 1964 to 1973 could be attributed to the changing social composition of the student test takers.[37] From 1973 to 1980, the percentage of decline attributable to changing populations was somewhat smaller.[38]

The third major charge that the inferential ability of seventeen-year-olds was declining has partial merit. Although this finding of the National Assessment for Progress holds true, it tells only part of the story. Whereas the authors of *A Nation at Risk* cite the decline, they fail to mention that the same study revealed that nine-year-olds' reading scores increased 3.8 percent.[39] This unevenness prompted Peter Peterson, a policy analyst with the liberal Brookings Institute, to claim that the data was deliberately misinterpreted to indicate negative findings.[40] Other critics concluded that *A Nation at Risk* was not a "reasoned treatise" but a "polemic," which carefully marshaled facts in order "to jar the public into action."[41]

However, two major charges made by the National Commission on Excellence in Education have more merit. First, American students have fallen behind in science achievement; a finding that might correlate with the difficulty of obtaining teachers in those areas, who tend to opt for more lucrative jobs in business. Second, there has been an alarming problem with illiteracy in America among low-income groups, the extent of which is still difficult to ascertain. In these respects, *A Nation at Risk* was on target, although it is debatable whether the charges justify the recommendations made by the National Commission.

There was some reason for critics to believe that the report's recommendations left much to be desired. The critics contend that there was little in the suggested reform items advanced that would strike at the heart of the alleged deterioration of public education. They held that those recommendations neglected two crucial aspects of the educational process: (1) strategies and techniques to improve pedagogy and (2) the financial resources needed to implement those reforms. As political scientist Aaron Wildavsky has observed, there can be no policy analysis without also determining the resources necessary to implement policy.[42] That determination *A Nation at Risk* failed to make. Instead, the report suggests five main recommendations. These include: (1) launching a core curriculum, designed mainly as college preparatory, "five new basics"; (2) raising academic standards in both public schools and colleges, focusing on raising criteria for college admissions; (3) lengthening the school day and school year in imitation of friendly foreign competitors; (4) raising teacher quality through certification tests and attracting capable teachers through the raising of salaries, mainly through the mechanism of merit pay; and (5) issuing a jeremiad to the public to hold their political leaders responsible for school reform, while also providing "the financial support necessary to accomplish these purposes."[43]

Of these recommendations, the weakest are lengthening of school day and year, and the institution of merit pay for teachers. Studies have shown that there is no significant correlation between time spent in school and academic achievement.[44] What appears more important is content of the material.[45] As for merit pay, it has proven a highly controversial issue and one that unites teachers in opposition.

A crucial flaw of *A Nation at Risk* was the lack of consideration for where the money would come from to enact reforms. The authors of the report announced that reform was the task of the states. Consequently, it would be the responsibility of state governments to flesh out the ideas with money. Even the policy analysts from the Heritage Foundation, in general agreement with *A Nation at Risk*, were wary of the implications. They commented that "policymakers do not have the luxury of treating costs so lightly" and that "improving education will, sooner or later, cost more money."[46] In a society newly conscious about an enormous federal deficit, there appeared problems with the states sharing the greater load of educational reform. With the federal government reducing outlays to states in order to reduce the national budget, "state budgets are often at the mercy of changes in federal policy," creating a gigantic Catch-22.[47] Moreover, raising state taxes would appear to be unlikely. Since the mid-1970s the trend has been for state governments to resist raising taxes under pressure from citizen groups. Such grass roots movements, such as Proposition 13 in California, succeeded in a number of states to reduce taxes.

One mechanism proposed by the American Enterprise Institute thinkers would be to shift the burden to the clients—students and parents. These thinkers suggest that student fees be collected in public school for activities such as band and athletics, as was done in California following the cuts in the school budget resulting from Proposition 13. It appears unlikely, however, that these alternatives could generate the massive revenue that would be needed to implement such suggestions as that of *A Nation at Risk*. Since 75 percent to 80 percent of a typical school budget is devoted to salaries, such recommendations as lengthening school day and year would be highly expensive. In short, *A Nation at Risk* is an educational policy without resources—not necessarily the best form of policy analysis.

Nevertheless, the commission sought widespread public approval for its report and its implications. Consequently, the commission members wrapped school reform in the American flag at a time when patriotic feeling bordered on chauvinism. *A Nation at Risk* appealed "to another dimension of the public's support" whose "best term to characterize it may simply be the honorable word 'patriotism.' "[48] This appeal came at a time when national feeling about America had resurged after decades of self-criticism during the sixties with the Vietnam War and the civil rights movement, and the seventies with Watergate. Mass culture revealed this conservative upswing. More people, mostly Americans, attended the 1984 Summer Olympics in Los Angeles than ever in history even though the Soviet bloc boycotted the games. The American public cheered on one United States victory after another. Films such as *Rambo, Rocky IV, Red Dawn,* and their imitators portrayed an oversimplified America combating the evils of communism and triumphing. Television commercials such as those made by Chrysler Chairman Lee Iacocca announced that "The Pride Is Back." The turning point could be ascribed to the election of Ronald Reagan in 1980, an event that neo-conservative sociologist Robert Nisbet would argue "could quite reasonably be seen as the glorious culmination of an ideological evolution that had begun three decades earlier."[49]

President Reagan would formally baptize the excellence movement in an address to the National Forum on Excellence in Education a few months after the publication of *A Nation at Risk*. Reagan proclaimed that "American schools don't need vast new sums of money as much as they need a few fundamental reforms."[50] Those include restoring "old fashioned discipline," raising academic standards, enhancing teacher quality and restoring parents "to their rightful place in the educational place."[51] Moreover, Reagan added that God "should never have been expelled from America's classrooms." And that school prayer should be once again permitted.[52]

The excellence movement would switch from equity to excellence. Perhaps the most acid critic of this goal transition was Professor Barbara Finkelstein of the University of Maryland. She criticized the excellence movement as a "retreat from historic visions of public education as an instrument of political democracy, a vehicle of social mobility."[53] She argued that the school reform movement of the 1960s had sought to "eliminate racism, ethnocentrism, ageism, sexism and sectarianism," whereas the 1980s excellence reform movement represented a "longing for fixed and enduring standards of conduct . . . (from) . . . a fear of economic impotence."[54] Finkelstein further maintained that the excellence reform movement entailed a change in values. According to her, instead of pursuing justice, egalitarianism and democratic principles, as was the case in the 1960s, the excellence reformers sought "technological productivity, military superiority, and cultural supremacy."[55]

## THE TEACHER UNIONS REACT

The teacher unions were upstaged by the excellence movement. The two unions had stressed essentially blue-collar labor issues since the teacher revolution in the 1960s.

Their concerns were primarily teacher salaries, working conditions and teacher rights. Scant attention was paid to educational issues and reform. David Selden, past president of the AFT, contends that the bitter rivalry between the unions to organize teachers left little time for educational concerns.[56] However, historically the main focus of the NEA had been professional issues, prior to the collective bargaining victory in 1961 in New York City. The resultant AFT militancy in organizing teachers in the big cities jolted the NEA out of its professional association stance to follow suit.

Whatever went beyond bread and butter goals was relegated to a lower priority. Consequently, school reform emerged from the strangest of quarters—the Reagan White House. The excellence movement's emphasis on the caliber of teaching, stiff academic standards and revamped curriculums caught the teacher unions off guard. The two teacher unions responded in differing fashions.

The NEA was more defensive. Suspicious of the excellence movement, their members' initial answer was to package "reforms" that, for the most part, resembled past demands. These included collecting more money to finance public education, strengthening the standards of schools of education and providing greater access to schooling.[57] These recommendations, made by an NEA Task Force on Educational Excellence in 1984, were silent on the issue of raising academic standards for both students and teachers. Later the NEA followed the AFT's lead in calling for teacher examinations for certification.

On the other hand, the NEA endorsed the objective of developing critical thinking and problem solving among students. And the official publication of the NEA, *NEA Today*, published forums on some issues raised by the excellence movement. Teachers took pro and con positions on such controversial questions as the desirability of a "core" curriculum, the need for community service for high school students (recommended by Boyer), the elimination of vocational education and the lengthening of the school year.[58]

Perhaps the most controversial issue for teachers was the suggestion from *A Nation at Risk*, endorsed by President Reagan, for merit pay. As proposed by merit pay–advocates, the basis of selecting certain teachers for additional monetary compensation would be the transfer of an ordinary business practice to public education. The better teachers would receive salary increases for higher performance. This step would be a measure of quality control. Furthermore, one side effect of merit pay–plans would be to attract more quality teachers. Not only would merit pay solve traditional low pay for public school teachers, it was argued, but it would, it was hoped, attract brighter students into the profession.

For some, merit pay is clearly an idea whose time has come. Indeed, President Reagan supported the concept in the 1984 presidental election. Moreover, Gallup polls in recent years had shown that six out of ten Americans favored merit pay–plans for teachers.[59] Clearly the concept of merit pay was one which was readily understandable.

The teacher unions have traditionally opposed the idea. They contend that plans for merit pay are difficult to implement, divisive and inappropriate for public education. Merit pay, it is argued, is difficult to determine because evaluating superior performance is too subjective. It is one thing to judge a college professor, they maintain, on the number of publications, committees served and student evaluations. There are no quantitative measures that can be used to evaluate public school teaching. Moreover, they contend, singling out a few for monetary rewards contributes to poor overall morale. And finally, it is maintained what may work for General Motors cannot be applied to a government monopoly.

The NEA was adamant in decrying merit pay. Don Cameron, executive director, stated that the single salary schedule did not "come about through a nefarious cabal of teacher advocates."[60] Rather, the system evolved as the one "best suited to accommodate the uniqueness of public school teachers."[61]

AFT President Albert Shanker, was equally opposed. After creating some confusion by inviting President Reagan to address the AFT convention in 1984 during the presidential campaign in order to discuss merit pay, Shanker reiterated labor's traditional complaint against merit pay:

To most teachers and their unions, merit pay does not suggest an incentive plan to improve knowledge and skills or to reward superior performance. It suggests the very antithesis of professionalism. . . . It means rewarding some teachers and demoralizing others on the basis of favoritism or politics. It means an excuse to keep overall teacher salaries low by giving one-time, largely symbolic bonuses to a few teachers under a quota system that sets a predetermined number of winners. . . . Teachers and their union do not object to thereby creating an incentive for all teachers to improve. Yet, throughout that same half century, we have continued to oppose merit pay because no such system we have ever seen or heard of has met those criteria. The result has been an unproductive stalemate between the public and teachers, two groups that should be natural allies.[62]

It was Shanker who was most in tune with the excellence movement and who became its leading teacher "cheerleader." In 1986 alone, Shanker devoted no less than a dozen of his paid weekly columns in the *New York Times* to school reform. Shanker issued a position paper in 1985 that would follow the lead of the excellence movement and restore "professionalism" to education.[63] The first order of business was raising the entry standards of teachers through a national examination. Somewhat reluctantly, the NEA weakly endorsed the need for national teacher certification. In addition, Shanker called for the creation of professional teacher boards that would develop standards, handle parent complaints and evaluate textbooks. These boards would be composed solely of teachers. Moreover, Shanker supported a variation of the voucher plan that had been esposed by an old foe, "old" reformer, Mario Fantini, dean of the School of Education at University of Massachusetts at Amherst.[64] Under the Fantini proposal, students could choose *only* public schools under federally funded vouchers. The pure voucher concept would encourage competition among public, private and parochial schools.

The professional image that Shanker projects is that of a teaching profession that borrows heavily from the practice of medicine. Doctors are experts, Shanker contends, who control standards, entry requirements and are not supervised. Teachers, on the other hand, lack the collegial relationship inherent in such professionalism. Shanker perceives the factory model to be most appropriate in describing teachers.

Shanker's allusion to the profession of medicine was not entirely on solid ground. The nature and historical structure of medicine has determined, in large measure, the nature of the profession, according to sociologist Paul Starr. In his classic study *The Social Transformation of Medicine,* Starr states that the failure of the federal government to regulate medicine prompted the American Medical Association to oversee the profession, and in turn, to play the largest role in the development of medical expertise.[65] On the other hand, public education is the province of government that regulates the industry. Consequently, unlike medicine, clients have little choice in who teaches their children.

Shanker's call for professionalism among American teachers signals a significant reversal in union policy. Whereas it was the NEA that historically touted professionalism and eschewed unionism, it was the old-line labor union reverting to its antagonist's former self. Shanker branded the NEA as being the most militant, having "discovered the confrontation of the 60s at a time when you've got to restore public confidence in American education by asserting professionalism."[66] Nevertheless, despite role reversal, the AFT still lags behind the NEA as a producer of research on educational issues. The quantity as well as quality of research publications on educational issues in the NEA dwarfs that of the AFT.

Shanker's factory model–analogy has more merit. Comparing teachers to workers in a class based society he holds that "schools are the last bastions of the rigid 19th century industrial hierarchy."[67] Shanker proposes a form of workplace democracy with greater input from teacher-workers along the style of the Theory Z participatory management of the Japanese. In this respect, he believes the Japanese system, with workers contributing to decision making and being rewarded with lifetime security, is one that American educators should imitate.

In his policy statement on professionalism, Shanker makes an eloquent appeal to his members to adopt his attitude. He signals a warning that the Reagan administration may not be friends of public education. Citing the proposing of tuition tax credits and vouchers by Reagan's policy aides, Shanker fears that the Reagan emphasis is on private education. Shanker alludes to the voucher system in Holland as transforming a largely public educational system into a private one. Moreover, he has witnessed the effects of cheaper competition on such basic industries as steel. "We are in the same situation as the steel and automobile industries 10 to 15 years ago," he declares. "They could see the tough competition that was coming, but they were unable to take action quickly enough."[68]

The bottom line, according to Shanker, is that the teachers, through their unions, have not been completely successful in bargaining for wages and working conditions. What the teachers must do now, he admonishes, is to build a "second revolution in American public education" that will go beyond collective bargaining to an era of enlightened professionalism. Teachers "have not been able to achieve all that we had hoped for through the bargaining process" so that we must now "go beyond collective bargaining to teacher professionalism: to succeed in preserving public education, and most important, improve" the status of teachers economically, socially and politically.[69]

In the end, Shanker, the consummate pragmatist, thinks in terms of power—*union* power. His major goal in the school reform movement is to redistribute educational power more into teacher union hands. He states in his agenda:

The only thing that's going to turn the schools around is to start turning over the decision making as to what works and what doesn't work over to the people who are actually doing the work and know what's happening in classrooms.

We ought to have the power to make the decisions because we *know more*—more about what is right and wrong to do in the education of children, more about what distinguishes a good textbook from a poor one, more about all of the issues in education.[70]

Shanker's remarks on professionalism received a good press. He was aware of the attention his comments made and with some pride proclaimed that "with the exception of *A Nation at Risk*, nothing in education in the past five or six years has gotten as much attention and editorial support as my proposals of a demanding national examination."[71]

There were some dissenters to this revival of professionalism. Professor Frank Riessman of Queens College in New York City and editor of the liberal journal *Social Policy* would charge that there was no evidence to show that more academically qualified teachers actually *"improve the learning of children."*[72] Riessman maintains that schools "are alien to their primary constituency, the students."[73] He suggests that rather than concentrating on teacher quality, one should adopt a student peer approach that would be both "empowering," and cost-effective.

## CONCLUSION

Government leaders have claimed that the excellence movement had turned around the alleged deterioration of the schools. Releasing a Department of Education study in 1986, Secretary William K. Bennett announced that the graduation rates increased in thirty-nine states from 1982 to 1984, and that there was a thirteen-point increase in SAT scores from 1982 to 1985. Bennett interpreted the results of the study as benefitting the twin goals of excellence and equity. "Some have said that we can't have both excellence and equity in the schools," he declared. "Clearly, raising standards and expectations for everyone means everyone benefits."[74]

The NEA, however, interpreted the study differently. NEA President Mary Futrell called the review "an incomplete picture of conditions in the nation's schools."[75] She found the study misleading. "We need an Education Department," she countered "that directly addresses the drop-out question, a great deal more than we need a department that congratulates itself over rising SAT scores."[76]

What impact has teacher unionism had on education? That is the ultimate question. On one level, the teacher union movement has had a necessary but incremental success in raising wages, improving working conditions, lobbying for educational legislation and, arguably, gaining more respect for teachers. On another level, teacher unionism has not become the engine for educational reform. Consequently, school reform emanated from the ideologically most conservative national administration in modern times.

Why has not educational reform emerged from the matrix of the teacher union movement, the largest and most powerful constituency in education? One answer, supplied by former president of AFT, David Selden, is that the inability to obtain teacher unity—one big teacher union—has hampered the concern for educational issues. According to Selden, since the early bargaining victories in the 1960s, the NEA and AFT have been too preoccupied with a bitter organizational rivalry to concentrate on educational reform.[77]

## NOTES

1. National Commission on Excellence in Education, *A Nation at Risk: The Imperative for Educational Reform* (Washington, D.C.: U.S. Government Printing Office, 1983), p. 5.

2. Beatrice Gross and Ronald Gross, eds., *The Great School Debate* (New York: Simon and Schuster, 1985), p. 15.

3. Chester E. Finn, Jr., "The Drive for Excellence: Moving Towards a Public Consensus," in Gross and Gross, *The Great School Debate*, p. 75.

4. Michael W. Kirst, "The Changing Balance in State and Local Power to Control Education," *Phi Delta Kappan*, November 1984, p. 189.

5. Ann Bastian et al., "The Mission of Schooling: Quality and Equality," *Christianity and Crisis*, March 18, 1985, p. 83.

6. David Selden, *The Teacher Rebellion* (Washington, D.C.: Howard University Press, 1985), p. 243.

7. U.S. Department of Education, "Responses to Reports from the Schools," in Gross and Gross, *The Great School Debate*, p. 393.

8. Ibid., p. 394.

9. Ibid., p. 392.

10. Chester E. Finn, Jr., *Education and the Presidency* (Lexington, Mass.: Lexington Books, 1977), p. 103.

11. Harold Howe II, "Education Moves to Center Stage: An Overview of Recent Studies," *Phi Delta Kappan,* November 1983, p. 171.

12. Maurice R. Berube, *Education and Poverty* (Westport, Conn.: Greenwood Press, 1984), p. 58.

13. Ibid., pp. 49-51.

14. Ibid., pp. 35-40.

15. Marvin Lazerson et al., *An Education of Value* (New York: Cambridge University Press, 1985), p. 49.

16. Ibid., p. xiii.

17. *A Nation at Risk,* p. 33.

18. Dennis P. Doyle and Terry W. Hartle, *Excellence in Education: The States Take Charge* (Washington, D.C.: American Enterprise Institute, 1985), p. 189.

19. Ibid.

20. Ibid., p. 22.

21. Ibid., p. i.

22. Finn, "The Drive for Excellence: Moving Towards a Public Consensus," p. 75.

23. Doyle and Hartle, *Excellence in Education: The States Take Charge,* p. 18.

24. Ibid.

25. Ibid.

26. Ibid., p. viii.

27. Ibid., p. 39.

28. *A Nation at Risk,* p. i.

29. Ibid., p. 5.

30. Ibid.

31. Ibid., p. 7.

32. Lawrence C. Steadman and Marshall S. Smith, "Weak Arguments, Poor Data, Simplistic Recommendations," in Gross and Gross, *The Great School Debate,* p. 88.

33. Torsten Husen, "Comparing the Incomparable," *Phi Delta Kappan,* March 1983, p. 455.

34. Steadman and Smith, "Weak Arguments, Poor Data, Simplistic Recommendations," p. 90.

35. *A Nation at Risk,* p. 13.

36. Husen, "Comparing the Incomparable," p. 460.

37. Steadman and Smith, "Weak Arguments, Poor Data, Simplistic Recommendations," p. 88.

38. Ibid.

39. Paul E. Peterson, "Did the Education Commissions Say Anything?" *Education and Urban Society,* February 1985, p. 128.

40. Ibid.

41. Steadman and Smith, "Weak Arguments, Poor Data, Simplistic Recommendations," p. 84.

42. Aaron Wildavsky, *Speaking Truth to Power: The Art and Craft of Policy Analysis* (Boston: Little, Brown, 1979), p. 21.

43. *A Nation at Risk,* p. 33.

44. Steadman and Smith, "Weak Arguments, Poor Data, Simplistic Recommendations," p. 97.

45. Ibid.

46. Doyle and Hartle, *Excellence in Education: The States Take Charge,* p. 42.

47. Ibid.

48. *A Nation at Risk,* p. 17.

49. Robert Nisbet, "The Conservative Renaissance in Perspective," *The Public Interest,* Fall 1985, p. 137.

50. Ronald Reagan, "The President's Address to the National Forum on Excellence in Education," *American Education,* March 1984, p. 2.

51. Ibid., p. 3.

52. Ibid.

53. Barbara Finkelstein, "Education and the Retreat From Democracy in the United States, 1979-198?," *Teachers College Record,* Winter 1984, pp. 276-77.

54. Ibid., p. 276.

55. Ibid., p. 277.

56. Telephone interview with David Selden, former president, American Federation of Teachers, AFL-CIO, Kalamazoo, Mich., February 12, 1986.

57. National Education Association, "NEA's Plan for School Reform," in Gross and Gross, *The Great School Debate,* pp. 405-10.

58. *NEA Today,* November 1983; January/February 1984; November 1984; June 1985.

59. Alec M. Gallup, "The 17th Annual Gallup Poll of the Public's Attitudes Toward the Public Schools," *Phi Delta Kappan,* September 1985, p. 39.

60. Don Cameron, "An Idea That Merits Consideration," *Phi Delta Kappan,* October 1985, p. 111.

61. Ibid.

62. Albert Shanker, "Separating the Wheat from the Chaff," *Phi Delta Kappan,* October 1985, p. 108.

63. Albert Shanker, *A Call for Professionalism* (Washington, D.C.: American Federation of Teachers, AFL-CIO, January 29, 1985).

64. It is instructive to note that Dr. Mario Fantini was the chief archi-

tect of the plan to obtain community controlled schools (elected boards) in New York City and a foe of Albert Shanker in that struggle. His book on vouchers, *Public Schools of Choice*, was published in 1973.

65. Paul Starr, *The Social Transformation of American Medicine* (New York: Basic Books, 1983).

66. *New York Times*, December 31, 1985, p. 7.

67. Shanker, *A Call for Professionalism*, p. 7.

68. Ibid., p. 5.

69. Ibid., pp. 2, 6.

70. Ibid., pp. 9, 12.

71. Ibid., p. 13.

72. Frank Riessman, "Why the New Professionalism in Education Won't Work," *Social Policy*, Fall 1985, p. 42.

73. Ibid.

74. *New York Times*, February 21, 1986, p. A10.

75. Ibid.

76. Ibid.

77. Interview with David Selden.

# 7

# Prospects for the Future

This study argues that the teacher unions have had substantive impacts in the political sphere. At the very least, the teacher unions have successfully developed sufficient political strength to halt such attempts at undermining public education as voucher plans and tuition tax credits. At most, the teacher unions have scored notable victories such as creating a separate Department of Education.

On balance, the teacher unions have been fairly effective representatives of education in politics; however, theirs has been primarily a watchdog role. The teacher unions have yet to become the *initiators* of sweeping educational change in America. Part of the reason for this defender role can be attributed to the time consumed in internecine conflict. Some observers, such as former AFT President David Selden, consider this organizational competition for members to be the chief cause of the lack of teacher union leadership in education.[1] They argue that the teacher unions need to be united into one organization to gain the security and added time to become a substantive educational agent of change. That appears to be the case.

Once, in its distant past, the NEA showed initiative in educational reform. At the beginning of its history in the late nineteenth century, the NEA would create prestigious committees to study educational questions. Undoubtedly the most influential of those was the Commission on the Reorganization of Secondary Education created in 1913 during the rise of the American high school. Unlike former committees that were composed of many college professors, the commission was made up mostly of school people. In the next eight years, the NEA commission would issue a number of reports on secondary education that would change the course of the high school.

The most significant of these reports was the *Cardinal Principles of Secondary Education* published in 1918. Prior committees, dominated by professors, reiterated the goal of high school education as essentially preparatory avenues for college. The *Cardinal Principles* enlarged the role of the high school. The purpose of high school, as perceived by the NEA commission, was to educate a diverse population, some of whom might *not* be destined for college. The *Cardinal Principles* enunciated seven objectives, including preparation for citizenship, family living, vocations, character development and acquiring basic skills. And so the all-purpose contemporary high school was born. The historian of the NEA's first century, Edgar B. Wesley, would proclaim that "probably no publication in the history of education ever surpassed . . . (the *Cardinal Principles*) . . . in importance, both because of its fundamental nature and because of its influence."[2]

Why has the NEA *not* followed in the same leadership role in education in the past generation? The evidence suggests that the NEA has been pre-occupied with organizational growth with the dawn of collective bargaining for teachers in 1961. In addition to the membership competition with the AFT, the NEA has also been pre-occupied with gaining political strength.

Although the teacher unions have been effective in their political objectives, one would be remiss in not mentioning the effects of collective bargaining in the public schools. Although consideration of the impact of collective bargaining is not a focus of this book, such consideration reveals a contrast to the political efforts of the teacher unions in search of obtaining their educational agenda. Until the present decade, there had been scant empirical research on the effect of teacher unionism on the public schools. That situation has been happily remedied, and a number of scholars have offered case studies on the effect of collective bargaining.

Their work indicates that collective bargaining may not necessarily have positive impacts and, sometimes, may have negative ones. First, William J. Grimshaw, in his 1979 study of the Chicago schools and the city political infrastructure, demonstrated that teacher unions have gained a measure of critical control over education. Examining the teacher's union and the power structure in Chicago, Grimshaw found that school administrators and school boards and elected public officials can only establish school policy when it conforms to union goals.

However, it was Randall W. Eberts and Joe A. Stone who mounted the most damaging evidence against collective bargaining. Their 1985 study examined 14,000 fourth graders in math from 328 elementary schools in a nationwide random sample. Adopting the production input-output research design, they factored in variables ranging from the socioeconomic background of pupils and parental involvement to teacher and principal characteristics and the amount of time spent on instruction. They concluded that students in union schools performed no better on the standardized math tests than did those in non-union schools.

Other evidence indicates mixed results. In her 1984 study of three militant union school districts, Susan Moore Johnson found both positive *and* negative impacts. On the one hand, collective bargaining resulted in class size–limits that made teaching easier, and the limitation of clerical duties enabled teachers to have more time for classroom preparation. On the other hand, collective bargaining did not increase a teacher's professional commitment nor did the inflexibility of class size–limits and rigid transfer policies prove educationally beneficial.

Finally in her 1985 study of three small, unionized school districts in southern New York State, Dorothy Kerr Jessup found similar conflicting impacts. In a 1979 follow-up of a 1969 survey, Jessup discovered that teachers were satisfied with the salary increases resulting from collective bargaining. Yet, they reported deteriorating job security and working conditions at a time of national retrenchment in education. Jessup concluded that the effectiveness of collective bargaining depended, to a large extent, on how the communities were receptive to teacher unionism.

## THE MEDICAL MODEL

Perhaps the next lesson for the teacher unions may be in uniting and becoming the agents for sweeping educational reform. In this respect, the teacher unions could profit by the example of the American Medical Association (AMA).

In their considerations of professionalism, teacher union leaders, among them AFT President Albert Shanker, have referred to medicine as a model for the teacher unions to follow.[3] An examination of medicine, and the role of the American Medical Association indicates that the AMA has succeeded in uniting the medical profession into *one* organization. Second, the AMA took the *initiative* in reforming medical education.

Founded in 1847, the AMA proclaimed two main goals: to unify the profession, and to elevate its qualitative standards. It succeeded in accomplishing both. Prior to the ascendency of the AMA, physicians were fragmented, and received poor medical education. Thus, the AMA initiated reform so that it raised "standards of medical education from the generally low levels of the nineteenth century to a position that no nation excelled or perhaps equaled."[4]

On the other hand, the AMA has contributed to a negative image of physicians in the last decade. By campaigning against access to care through such federal programs as national health insurance and Medicare and Medicaid, the AMA projected an image of a physician who was theoretically opposed to "socialized medicine" but actually more concerned with limitations upon his/her income. Consequently, public perceptions of physicians were negative; there was even a corresponding decline in AMA membership in the early 1970s.[5]

The medical profession developed differently in the United States. Physicians were free-market entrepreneurs who enjoyed freedom from federal controls. In the nineteenth century, the states created licensing boards, but it was many years before they imposed rigorous standards. There were numerous "quack" practitioners and "quack" remedies. Still, the AMA strongly believed "the greatest threat to professional security (to be) the national government."[6]

Perhaps the chief accomplishment of the AMA was its role in improving medical education. In 1904, the AMA created a Council on Medical Education, composed of professors of medicine at major universities.[7] The professors would examine the standards at the medical schools. The council conducted a survey two years later and concluded that only 82 of the 160 medical schools were adequate.[8] The AMA reported the results at one of its meetings but refrained from making them public, since professional ethics forbid physicians from taking cudgels against each other.[9] Instead, the AMA sought outside support. The organization turned to the Carnegie Foundation for the Advancement for Teaching. The foundation chose a young educator, a layman, Abraham Flexner, to investigate once again the quality of education at the medical schools.

Flexner severely criticized most of the medical schools. Their abuses were rife. Some schools had no laboratories; others had no libraries; student admissions standards were waived if the applicant could pay; some professors were engaged in private practice. In short, "America had some of the world's best medical schools but also many of the worst."[10] Flexner concluded that the better schools should be strengthened and the weak ones eliminated. He advocated that only 31 of the 160 medical schools should survive.[11]

Concomitantly, state licensing boards were raising their standards, causing economic hardship for some schools. New state requirements extending medical education made medical school an increasingly expensive proposition. Since some private schools could not subsidize medical education, they closed. Nevertheless, the Flexner report, according to sociologist Paul Starr, "hastened the schools [demise]."[12] What is important for the teacher unions is that the AMA took the initiative in reforming its own profession.

Paradoxically, the AMA may be moving more toward becoming a union when the teachers are moving toward professionalism. First, the AMA shored up its lobbying effort in 1961 with a political action committee (AMPAC) that would support political candidates.[13] Second, and most important, the structure of medicine has changed. It has shifted from an entrepreneurial system, with the doctor as sole practitioner, to corporate and group practice. The corporations have perceived huge profits to be derived in health care and have invested in health maintenance organizations where the physician is an employee. With medical unemployment widespread in Western Europe and Latin America, there is a corresponding oversupply of physicians in the United States. James Sammons, executive vice president of the AMA, foresees the AMA eventually becoming a bargaining agent for these physicians in hospitals and health maintenance organizations.[14] And finally, AMA membership nowhere matches that of the two teacher unions. Only 48 percent of the men physicians and only 26 percent of the women belong to the AMA.[15]

## MERGER

In order for the teacher unions to have maximum political and educational impact, one concludes that they must merge into one powerful organization. Together they would possess immense combined financial and political import. The bitter organizational rivalry has left the teacher unions with too little time to concentrate on educational reform.

The merger of the NEA and AFT would have a dramatic impact. Professor Myron Lieberman perceived this potential over a decade ago. He welcomed a merger of the two unions as a "major power base in American society."[16] Writing at the height of the merger fever in the early 1970s, Lieberman conjured a prescient scenario for the 1980 Democratic national convention. By that time, Lieberman mused, a merged teacher union would swing the needed convention delegates to Walter Mondale. The major educational campaign pledge would be for the federal government to assume one half of all educational spending. In fact the NEA was instrumental in swinging the nomination to Carter *and* Mondale in 1980, and to Mondale in 1984.[17] Moreover, the NEA goal has been for one-third assumption of educational costs by the federal government.

Even the opponents of merger comprehend the political advantage of one big union. For example, Ken Nielsen, who opposed David Selden unsuccessfully for the AFT presidency in 1972, conceded, that "Congress might better respond to one unified organization."[18] Some friends of education felt otherwise. Stanley E. Elam, longtime editor of the prestigious educational journal, *Phi Delta Kappan*, worried that merger would produce "the most powerful white collar union in America" and wondered whether that would "truly serve the public interest."[19]

The chief advocate for merger has been David Selden. Selden wanted the creation of one big teacher union that would be the cutting edge of educational and social reform. He came to this conclusion after his success in merging rival teacher groups in New

York City, which resulted in 1961 in the first collective bargaining election for teachers nationally. Selden believed that "the entire educational system would have to be renovated and reconstructed."[20] That was his main reason for "advocating teacher unity."[21] Moreover, according to Selden, "a united teacher organization was essential for building a liberal labor political force similar to those which functioned in most European countries."[22]

With the ascent of Selden to the AFT presidency in 1968, the merger fever began. In his nominating speech at the AFT convention, Selden boldly made teacher unity his priority. Until his defeat by Albert Shanker in 1974, Selden assiduously pursued a merger between the teacher unions, and he came close to accomplishing his goal. The NEA and AFT had four serious negotiating sessions on merger in those years. However, within the ranks of both unions the opponents of merger won out.

The NEA had most to lose with merger. The larger and more powerful organization, members were fearful lest the smaller AFT, with its organizational skills, bore from within and capture the merged union. Consequently, the NEA foresaw major obstacles to merger. First, and foremost, the NEA was reluctant to affiliate with the AFL-CIO. The NEA leadership distrusted the aims and philosophy of the AFL-CIO. Second, NEA officials wanted a secret ballot for the election of officers of the merged unit. They were concerned that the smaller AFT might capture the leadership positions. There was some cause for alarm on that point. Myron Lieberman, for example, would speculate that the "dominant leader . . . might surely be Albert Shanker."[23] And lastly, the NEA wanted to retain its preferential election procedures, which guarantee minority candidates leadership positions. The AFT had denounced the practice as filling quotas.

Another major obstacle to a merger was the growing stature of AFT President Albert Shanker. Shanker was considered by some NEA officials as a "political opportunist interested primarily in amassing power."[24]

There were several local mergers of NEA and AFT affiliates during the merger era. In 1969, AFT and NEA affiliates merged in Flint, Michigan. The next year, the teacher unions merged in Los Angeles. But the most significant breakthrough occurred in New York State in 1972. Lieberman speculated that that merger would have "the most profound effects not only in teacher organizations and education but in labor relations and politics as well."[25] By 1976, the promising New York State breakthrough was a fizzle. The NEA withdrew from the merged unit.

On a national level, the NEA responded to David Selden's merger overture. In 1969, NEA President George Fischer discussed merger plans with AFT's Selden. At the time, a poll of teachers indicated that two-thirds believed a merger of the NEA and AFT would prove beneficial to the AFT but not to the NEA.[26] In addition, a majority believed that teachers would *not* benefit from a merger.[27] Despite the lack of grass roots teacher support, Selden was optimistic that the NEA would want to merge once the AFT grew in numbers to at least 250,000 members.[28]

The stumbling block was AFL-CIO affiliation. Selden was able to obtain a waiver on that issue from Lane Kirkland, then Secretary-Treasurer of the AFL-CIO. Kirkland agreed with Selden that the merger of the two teacher unions was "so important" that the barrier of AFL-CIO affiliation should not remain.[29] Four meetings between NEA and AFT officials were scheduled. In the final analysis, the NEA withdrew from the talks in 1974, and the merger issue was dead.[30]

One reason Selden made headway in merger talks was his more balanced view of his rival, the NEA. According to Selden, he had not "developed the hatred of the NEA that many other union activists felt," since he believed that the NEA benefited "teachers through its research, its advocacy of state and federal aid to education and its liberal attitude toward most educational policy issues."[31]

On the other hand, Selden's successor, Albert Shanker, did not share these views. Over the years Shanker devoted nine columns in his paid advertisement in the *New York Times* attacking the NEA on issues ranging from teacher unity to alleged pro-communist views. Shanker wrote three columns on teacher unity during the prospects for merger. Essentially he upheld the need for AFL-CIO affiliation. "Teachers are quickly learning," he wrote in 1974, after the collapse of the merger talks, "that in the months and years to come they will need the support, both political and economic, of organized labor."[32]

Still, Shanker perceived the political implications of a merged teacher union. For one thing, teacher unity would facilitate organizing the 1.5 million unorganized teachers into a union well over 3 million members—by far, the largest union in America. And Shanker foresaw the political power that would attend such a union:

The number alone is impressive; but the power and influence of such an organization would have been magnified by its vast geographic spread. It would have claimed members in ever political election district in the nation.[33]

Merger was an idea whose time had come, and gone. No new merger initiatives have been offered since the Selden era. One cannot blame solely the hard-liners of the AFT, for the failure to realize a course that appears logical to most teacher union observers. Surely, the NEA leadership was equally recalcitrant.

Still, one must conclude that the future of the NEA and AFT as more powerful political and educational institutions resides with merger. Perhaps, only then will the teacher unions fully realize their potential and become the engine for educational reform that they must be in order to fulfill their destiny.

## NOTES

1. Telephone interview with David Selden, former President, American Federation of Teachers, AFL-CIO, Kalamazoo, Mich., February 12, 1986.

2. Edgar B. Wesley, *NEA: The First Hundred Years* (New York: Harper and Bros., 1957), p. 75.

3. Albert Shanker, *The Making of a Profession* (Washington, D.C.: American Federation of Teachers, AFL-CIO, April, 1985).

4. James G. Burrow, *AMA: Voice of American Medicine* (Baltimore, Md.: Johns Hopkins Press, 1963), p. 317.

5. Paul Starr, *The Social Transformation of American Medicine* (New York: Basic Books, 1982), p. 379.

6. Burrow, *AMA: Voice of American Medicine*, p. 153.

7. Starr, *The Social Transformation of American Medicine*, p. 117.

8. Ibid., p. 118.

9. Ibid.

10. Ibid., p. 120.

11. Ibid.

12. Ibid.

13. Frank D. Campion, *The AMA and U.S. Health Policy Since 1940* (Chicago: Chicago Review Press, 1984), p. 215.

14. Ibid., p. 427.

15. Ibid.

16. Myron Lieberman, "The Union Merger Movement: Will 3,500,000 Teachers Put It All Together?" *Saturday Review*, June 24, 1972, p. 52.

17. Ibid.

18. Ibid., p. 55.

19. Stanley E. Elam, "Teachers in Politics and the Merger Issue," *Phi Delta Kappan*, October 1976, p. 154.

20. David Selden, *The Teacher Rebellion* (Washington, D.C.: Howard University Press, 1985),p. 131.

21. Ibid.

22. Ibid.

23. Lieberman, "The Union Merger Movement," p. 52.

24. Kenneth P. Lubetsky, "Will the NEA and the AFT Ever Merge?" *The Educational Forum*, 41 (March 1977), p. 314.

25. Myron Lieberman, "NEA-AFT Merger: Breakthrough in New York," *Phi Delta Kappan*, June 1972, p. 622.

26. "AFT/NEA Merger?" *Instructor*, March 1970, p. 43.

27. Ibid.

28. Selden, *The Teacher Rebellion*, p. 132.

29. Ibid., p. 136.

30. Lubetsky, "Will the NEA and the AFT Ever Merge?" p. 312.

31. Selden, *The Teacher Rebellion*, p. 125.

32. Albert Shanker, "Now, More than Ever, Teachers Need Unity and Labor Support," *New York Times*, May 12, 1974, p. E11.

33. Albert Shanker, "Teacher Unity: Present Hopes Dashed . . . " *New York Times*, March 3, 1974, p. E7.

# Bibliography

## BOOKS

Berube, Maurice R. *Education and Poverty: Effective Schooling in the United States and Cuba.* Westport, Conn.: Greenwood Press, 1984.

Berube, Maurice R., and Marilyn Gittell, eds. *Confrontation at Ocean Hill–Brownsville.* New York: Praeger, 1969.

Blumenfeld, Samuel L. *NEA: Trojan Horse in American Education.* Boise, Idaho: Paradigm, 1984.

Boyer, Ernest et al. *High School.* New York: Harper and Row, 1983.

Braun, Robert J. *Teachers and Power: The Story of the American Federation of Teachers.* New York: Simon and Schuster, 1972.

Burrow, James G. *AMA: Voice of American Medicine.* Baltimore, Md.: Johns Hopkins Press, 1963.

Campion, Frank D. *The AMA and U.S. Health Policy Since 1940.* Chicago: Chicago Review Press, 1984.

Cresswell, Anthony M., and Michael Murphy, with Charles T. Kerchner. *Teachers, Unions, and Collective Bargaining in Education.* Berkeley, Calif.: McCuthan, 1980.

Doyle, Dennis P., and Terry W. Hartle. *Excellence in Education: The States Take Charge.* Washington, D.C.: American Enterprise Institute, 1985.

Eaton, William Edward. *The American Federation of Teachers, 1916-1961.* Carbondale: Southern Illinois University Press, 1975.

Eberts, Randall W., and Joe A. Stone. *Unions and Public Schools: The Effect of Collective Bargaining on American Education.* Lexington, Mass.: Lexington Books, 1983.

Elmore, Richard F., and Milbrey Wallin McLaughlin. *Reform and Re-trenchment: The Politics of California School Finance Reform.* Cambridge, Mass.: Ballinger, 1982.

Fantini, Mario. *Public Schools of Choice.* New York: Simon and Schuster, 1973.

Finn, Chester E., Jr. *Education and the Presidency.* Lexington, Mass.: Lexington, Books, 1977.

Gittell, Marilyn, with Maurice R. Berube et al. *Local Control in Education.* New York: Praeger, 1972.

———. *School Boards and School Policy.* New York: Praeger, 1973.

Grimshaw, William J. *Union Rule in the Schools.* Lexington, Mass.: Lexington Books, 1979.

Gross, Beatrice, and Ronald Gross, eds. *The Great School Debate.* New York: Simon and Schuster, 1985.

Herndon, Terry. *We, The Teachers: Terry Herndon on Education and Democracy.* Cabin John, Md.: Seven Locks Press, 1983.

Jessup, Dorothy Kerr. *Teachers, Unions and Change: A Comparative Study.* New York: Praeger, 1985.

Johnson, Susan Moore. *Teacher Unions in Schools.* Philadelphia: Temple University Press, 1984.

Kirst, Michael W. *Who Controls Our Schools?* New York: W. H. Freeman, 1984.

Lazerson, Marvin et al. *An Education of Value.* New York: Cambridge University Press, 1985.

Lerner, Barbara. *Minimum Competence, Maximum Choice.* New York: Irvington, 1980.

Miringoff, Lee M., and Barbara L. Carvalho. *The Cuomo Factor: Assessing the Political Appeal of New York's Governor.* Poughkeepsie, N.Y.: Marist Institute for Public Opinion, 1986.

Ravitch, Diane. *The Troubled Crusade: American Education 1945-1980.* New York: Basic Books, 1983.

Rosenthal, Alan, and Susan Fuhrman. *Legislative Education Leadership in the States.* Washington, D.C.: Institute for Educational Leadership, 1981.

Sabato, Larry J. *PAC Power: Inside the World of Political Action Committees.* New York: W. W. Norton, 1984.

Selden, David. *The Teacher Rebellion.* Washington, D.C.: Howard University Press, 1985.

Starr, Paul. *The Social Transformation of American Medicine.* New York: Basic Books, 1982.

Taft, Philip. *United They Teach: The Story of the United Federation of Teachers.* Los Angeles: Nash Publishing, 1974.

Waxman, Chaim I. *The Stigma of Poverty*. New York: Pergamon Press, 1983.

Wesley, Edgar B. *NEA: The First Hundred Years*. New York: Harper and Bros., 1957.

West, Allan M. *The National Education Association: The Power Base for Education*. New York: Free Press, 1980.

White, Theodore. *America in Search of Itself: The Making of the President, 1956-1980*. New York: Harper and Row, 1982.

Wildavsky, Aaron. *Speaking Truth to Power: The Art and Craft of Policy Analysis*. Boston: Little, Brown, 1979.

## REPORTS AND UNPUBLISHED MATERIAL

American Federation of Teachers, AFL-CIO. *A Guide to Political Action*. Washington, D.C., September 1981.

———. *Guide for Legislative Action and State Collective Bargaining Laws*. Washington, D.C., 1975.

———. *Register and Vote: The Future Depends on It*. Washington, D.C., 1984.

———. *Voting Record 1984: The AFT Rates the 98th Congress*. Washington, D.C., 1985.

———. *Voting Record 1986: The AFT Rates the 99th Congress*. Washington, D.C., 1986.

Gittell, Marilyn, with Maurice R. Berube et al. *School Decentralization and School Policy in New York City*. New York: Institute for Community Studies, 1971.

Johns, Harold. "The National Teachers Examination—A Closer Look." Norfolk, Va., 1986.

National Commission on Excellence in Education. *A Nation at Risk: The Imperative for Educational Reform*. Washington, D.C.: U.S. Government Printing Office, 1983.

National Education Association. *How To Endorse Candidates*. Washington, D.C., 1986.

———. *How To Participate in Party Politics*. Washington, D.C., 1981.

———. *How To Raise Money for NEA-PAC: Education's Defense Fund*. Washington, D.C., March 1985.

———. *How To Recruit, Organize, and Manage Volunteers*. Washington, D.C., 1982.

———. *How To Run Voter Contact Programs*. Washington, D.C., 1982.

———. *How To Set Up and Operate a Local Association Political Action Program*. Washington, D.C., August 1985.

———. *Rankings of the States 1986*. Washington, D.C., August 1986.

————. *The NEA Legislative Program for the 99th Congress.* Washington, D.C., July 1985.

————. *The Radical Right Attack on the National Education Association.* Washington, D.C., March 1985.

————. *You and Politics: A Workbook Introduction* (Trainer's Guide). Washington, D.C., March 1985.

Public Education Association. *Community School Board Election: Candidates List, May 6, 1986—An Annotated List.* New York, 1986.

Pullen, Dale. *The U.S. Congress Handbook, 1986, 99th Congress.* McLean, Va., 1986.

Shanker, Albert. *A Call for Professionalism.* Washington, D.C.: American Federation of Teachers, AFL-CIO, January 29, 1985.

————. *The Making of a Profession.* Washington, D.C.: American Federation of Teachers, AFL-CIO, April 1985.

Shotts, Constance Trisler. "The Origin and Development of the National Education Association Political Action Committee 1969–1976." Ann Arbor, Mich.: Xerox University Microfilms, 1976.

Union of Concerned Scientists. *Choices: A Unit on Conflict and Nuclear War.* Washington, D.C.: National Education Association, 1983.

## ARTICLES

Apple, R. W., Jr. "The Question of Mario Cuomo." *New York Times Magazine,* September 14, 1986.

American Federation of Teachers, AFL-CIO. "Bakke: Pro and Con." *Phi Delta Kappan,* March 1978.

Bastian, Ann et al. "The Mission of Schooling: Quality and Equality." *Christianity and Crisis,* March 18, 1985.

Boyton, Bill, and John Lloyd. "Why the Largest Teachers Union Puts Its Staff First and Education Second." *Washington Monthly,* May 1985.

Berube, Maurice R. "Democratic Socialists and the Schools." *New Politics,* Summer 1969.

————. "The Trouble with Vouchers." *Commonweal,* January 29, 1971.

Chapman, Steven. "The Teachers' Coup." *New Republic,* October 11, 1980.

Cohen, David K., and Eleanor Farrar. "Power to the Parents: The Story of Education Vouchers." *Public Interest,* Summer 1977.

Cramer, Jerome. "Here's How Teacher Power Affects You." *The American School Board Journal,* November 1980.

Dewing, Rolland. "The NEA and Minority Rights." *The Journal of Negro Education,* Fall 1978.

Elam, Stanley E. "Educators and the Nuclear Threat." *Phi Delta Kappan,* April 1983.

———. "Teachers in Politics and the Merger Issue." *Phi Delta Kappan,* October 1976.

Finkelstein, Barbara. "Education and the Retreat from Democracy in the United States 1979-198?" *Teachers College Record,* Winter 1984.

Finn, Chester E., Jr. "Teacher Politics." *Commentary,* February 1983.

———. "Teacher Unions and School Quality: Potential Allies or Inevitable Foes?" *Phi Delta Kappan,* January 1985.

Futrell, Mary Hatwood. "An Educator's Opinion" (Column). *Washington Post.*

———. "New Report, Old Truths." *Education Week,* May 28, 1986.

———. "Vouchers: The Hoax Is Transparent." *Washington Post,* December 15, 1985.

Gallup, Alec M. "The Gallup Poll of Teacher Attitudes Toward the Public Schools." *Phi Delta Kappan,* October 1984.

———. "The 17th Annual Gallup Poll of the Public's Attitudes Toward the Public Schools." *Phi Delta Kappan,* September 1985.

Gallup, George. "The 16th Annual Gallup Poll of the Public's Attitudes Toward the Public Schools." *Phi Delta Kappan,* September 1984.

Heisner, J. D. "Teachers Helped Put Them There: Now Carter and Mondale Are Accountable, Too." *Instructor,* January 1977.

Herndon, Terry. "A Teacher Speaks of Peace." *Phi Delta Kappan,* April 1983.

———. "Reply to Reader's Digest." *Phi Delta Kappan,* February 1979.

Higgins, George V. "Challenging the Kennedy 'Magic.' " *New York Times Magazine,* August 3, 1986.

Howe, Harold, II. "Education Moves to Center Stage: An Overview of Recent Studies." *Phi Delta Kappan,* November 1983.

Husen, Torsten. "Comparing the Incomparable." *Phi Delta Kappan,* March 1983.

Jaschik, Scott. "On New York Campuses, Cuomo Draws Strong Support, Vociferous Criticism." *The Chronicle of Higher Education,* September 17, 1986.

Kaplan, George R. "Shining Lights in High Places: Education's Top Four Leaders and Their Heirs." *Phi Delta Kappan,* September 1985.

Kirk, Russell. "The NEA Plans Our Future." *National Review,* November 11, 1976.

———. "Trouble for the NEA." *National Review,* October 7, 1980.

Kirst, Michael W. "The Changing Balance in State and Local Power to Control Education." *Phi Delta Kappan,* November 1984.

Krathwohl, David R. "The National Teacher Examination and Professional Standards." *Educational Leadership*, February 1983.

Lieberman, Myron. "The Union Merger Movement: Will 3,500,000 Teachers Put It All Together?" *Saturday Review*, June 24, 1972.

Lubetsky, Kenneth P. "Will the NEA and the AFT Ever Merge?" *The Educational Forum*, March 1977.

McGuire, Willard. "Labor as a National Movement." *Today's Education*, September 1981.

———. "Politics 1980." *NEA Today*, February-March 1980.

McLauglin, Milbrey W., and James Catterall. "Notes on the New Politics of Education." *Education and Urban Society*, May 1984.

Mercer, Walter. "The Gathering Storm: Teacher Testing and Black Teachers." *Educational Leadership*, February 1983.

Methvin, Eugene H. "Guess Who Spells Disaster for Education?" *Reader's Digest*, May 1984.

———. "The NEA: A Washington Lobby Run Rampant." *Reader's Digest*, November 1978.

National Education Association. "Bakke: Pro and Con." *Phi Delta Kappan*, March 1978.

Neill, George. "NEA: New Powerhouse in the Democratic Party." *Phi Delta Kappan*, October 1980.

Nisbet, Robert. "The Conservative Renaissance in Perspective." *The Public Interest*, Fall 1985.

Peterson, Paul E. "Did the Education Commissions Say Anything?" *Education and Urban Society*, February 1985.

Reagan, Ronald. "The President's Address to the National Forum on Excellence in Education." *American Education*, March 1984.

Riessman, Frank. "Why the New Professionalism in Education Won't Work." *Social Policy*, Fall 1985.

Shanker, Albert. "Education and Politics: Emerging Alliances." *Educational Leadership*, November 1976.

———. "Mondale Is the Right Choice." *American Teacher*, May 1984.

———. "Separating the Wheat from the Chaff." *Phi Delta Kappan*, October 1985.

———. *Where We Stand*. (Column), *New York Times:* "Teacher Unity: Present Hopes Dashed . . . " March 3, 1974.

———. "Now, More Than Ever, Teachers Need Unity—And Labor Support." May 12, 1974.

———. "High Court Bakke Ruling: A Mixed Bag." July 9, 1978.

———. "64% Reject Private School Tuition Aid." August 6, 1978.

———. "NEA Endorse Soviet Propaganda." December 10, 1978.

————. "No Reason for Separate Education Department." March 4, 1979.

————. "If You Love New York, Vote for Kennedy." March 23, 1980.

————. "No, I'm Not Sorry I Supported Kennedy." August 17, 1980.

————. "How Not To Teach About the KKK." November 1, 1981.

————. "Holland's Public Education Vanishing." July 4, 1982.

————. "NEA Trying to Teach—Or Indoctrinate?" April 17, 1983.

————. "Will Testing Knock Out Minorities?" May 19, 1985.

————. "When Testing Teachers May Be Hoax." July 21, 1985.

————. "Sometimes the Administration Is Right." October 13, 1985.

————. "Voucher Proposal: Nose of the Camel." November 17, 1985.

Sullam, Brian. "The NEA Discovers the Ballot." *Nation*, April 24, 1976.

Wicker, Tom. "20 Down Hill Years." *New York Times*, June 18, 1985.

Winkler, Karen J. "Precipitous Decline of American Unions Fuels Growing Interest Among Scholars." *Chronicle of Higher Education*, November 12, 1986.

## NEWSPAPERS, MAGAZINES, AND NEWSLETTERS

*American School Board Journal*, September 1975 and November 1980.

*American Teacher*, April 1917, September 1980, December/January 1983-84, and October 1986.

*Commonweal*, May 6, 1983.

*Instructor*, March 1970.

*London Times Educational Supplement*, January 9, 1976, and July 13, 1984.

*NEA Today*, November 1983, January/February 1984, November 1984, June 1985, and December 1985.

*Phi Delta Kappan*, October 1976.

*New York Teacher*, September 29, 1986.

*New York Times*, January 15, 1975; June 3, 1985; July 2, 1985; January 2, 1986; February 8, 1986; April 27, 1986; May 9, 1986; May 16, 1986; May 24, 1986; May 25, 1986; July 3, 1986; July 7, 1986; July 8, 1986; August 18, 1986; August 31, 1986; September 10, 1986; September 16, 1986; October 4, 1986; October 17, 1986; October 25, 1986; October 27, 1986; October 28, 1986; November 6, 1986; November 7, 1986; November 8, 1986; November 20, 1986; December 17, 1986; and January 25, 1987.

*Save our Schools Newsletter*, May 1985.

*Time*, July 12, 1976.

*Today's Education*, February/March 1980, and September 1981.

*Virginia Ledger-Star*, April 11 and August 12, 1986.

*Washington Post*, September 11 and October 29, 1986.

## INTERVIEWS

Bonner, Guessippina, Political Specialist, Massachusetts Teachers Association, Boston, Mass. August 28, 1986 (By phone).

Carter, Beulah, Staff Assistant, Research Department, AFL-CIO, Washington, D.C. November 14, 1986 (By phone).

Conway, John, Congressional Contact Team Coordinator, National Education Association, Washington, D.C. February 13, 1987 (By phone).

Dorfer, Rolland, Regional Lobbyist, National Education Association, Norfolk, Va. October 14, 1985.

Hill, Michael, Legislative Director for Congressman Dave Kildee (D-Mich.), Washington, D.C. September 3, 1986 (By phone).

Horowitz, Rachelle, Director of Committee on Political Education (COPE), American Federation of Teachers, AFL-CIO, Washington, D.C. December 3, 1986 (By phone).

Humphrey, Gregory, Director of Legislation, American Federation of Teachers, AFL-CIO, Washington, D.C. December 3, 1986 (By phone).

Lestina, Dale, Manager of Governmental Relations Special Projects, National Education Association, Washington, D.C. June 16, 1986; September 22, 1986 (By phone).

Lyons, Kathleen, Political Specialist, Maryland State Teachers Association, Baltimore, Md. September 3, 1986 (By phone).

Marlowe, Deanna, Legislative Aide to Senator Mark Andrews (R-N.D.) Washington, D.C. September 12, 1986 (By phone).

Matts, Sharon, Administrative Assistant to Congressman Jack Brooks (D-Texas), Washington, D.C. September 12, 1986 (By phone).

Miller, Dr. Yvonne, Assemblywoman, Virginia State Assembly, Norfolk, Va. November 25, 1985.

Morris, Gerald, Associate Director of Legislation, American Federation of Teachers, AFL-CIO, Washington, D.C. December 1, 1986 (By phone).

Powell, Dave, Publications Officer, National Education Association, Washington, D.C. April 24, 1986 (By phone).

Selden, David, former President, American Federation of Teachers, AFL-CIO, Kalamazoo, Mich. February 12, 1986 (By phone).

Shulz, Amy, Legislative Aide to U.S. Senator Quentin Burdick (D-N.D.), Washington, D.C. September 8, 1986 (By phone).

Skuse, Ray, Director of Political Affairs, New York State United Teachers, AFL-CIO, Albany, N.Y. June 21, 1985 (By phone).

Standa, Joseph, Political Affairs Specialist, National Education Association, Washington, D.C. June 2, 1985; October 20, 1986 (By phone); and November 14, 1986 (By phone).

## LETTERS AND MEMORANDUMS

Horowitz, Rachelle, Director of Committee on Political Education (COPE), American Federation of Teachers, AFL-CIO. Letter to Donna Horton, National Commission on Election Information, Washington, D.C., October 17, 1984.
————. Memorandum to AFT Executive Council and COPE Liaisons, Washington, D.C., March 11, 1985.
Kirkland, Lane, President AFL-CIO. Memorandum to Affiliated Local Central Bodies, Washington, D.C., November 27, 1984.
National Education Association. Memorandum NEA-PAC Endorsement-Election Report: 1986 Election Cycle, Washington, D.C., November 11, 1986.

## PRESS RELEASES

Corelle, Beverly L. President, Maryland State Teachers Association, 1986 Representative Assembly Recommends Michael Barnes for U.S. Senate. Baltimore, Md., Press Release, April 19, 1986.

## TELEVISION

League of Women Voters. "The 8th Congressional Primary Election Debate," Boston, Mass. Television, C-Span, September 2, 1986.

# Index

**About the Author**

MAURICE R. BERUBE is Associate Professor of Education at Old Dominion University. He is the author of *Education and Poverty: Effective Schooling in the United States and Cuba* (Greenwood Press, 1984) and *The Urban University in America* (Greenwood Press, 1978); co-author of *School Boards and School Policy* (Praeger, 1973) and *Local Control in Education* (Praeger, 1972); and co-editor of *Confrontation at Ocean Hill–Brownsville* (Praeger, 1969). His articles have been published in *The Urban Review, Social Policy, Commonweal, The Nation, New Politics, Cross Currents,* and other journals.